BABYSITTING GEORGE

BABYSITTING GEORGE

GEORGE

Celia Walden

BLOOMSBURY

LONDON • BERLIN • NEW YORK • SYDNEY

First published in Great Britain 2011

Copyright © by Celia Walden 2011

The moral right of the author has been asserted

Bloomsbury Publishing Plc
36 Soho Square
London W1D 3QY

www.bloomsbury.com

Bloomsbury Publishing, London, New York and Berlin
A CIP catalogue record for this book is available from the British Library

ISBN 978 1 4088 1417 8

10 9 8 7 6 5 4 3 2 1

Typeset by Hewer Text UK Ltd, Edinburgh
Printed in Great Britain by Clays Ltd, St Ives plc

MIX
Paper from
responsible sources
FSC® C018072
FSC
www.fsc.org

To my brothers, Oliver and Frank

'We're all in the gutter, but some of us are looking at the stars.'

– Oscar Wilde

A NOTE TO THE READER

IN THE TEN YEARS I've worked as a journalist, no job has marked me more than the first I was sent on: the job of babysitting George Best. At the time, I remember thinking that the car chases with the paparazzi, hasty back-door exits and blonde mistresses involved were the stuff of films; that it would be impossible to explain the warped relationship between the press and celebrities to anyone outside the media.

Now, years later, I have tried to do just that. This isn't a football book, nor is it a biography charting the rise and fall of one of Britain's best-loved sportsmen. *Babysitting George* is a personal memoir of the scorching summer of 2003 based on the fragmented encounters of a naïve young journalist with a dying star. Our conversations have been replicated as faithfully as possible from memory, notes and tapes, as have the events of that period. For clarity the various people I reported to have been collectively referred to as 'my boss' or 'the boss'. I hope that the picture of George that emerges is a fond one. It is certainly intended to be.

Celia Walden

PROLOGUE

IT DOESN'T TAKE LONG for the jokes to start. Not in the newsroom of a national paper.

'You heard the one about George Best? He's in an airport with the Man U team, right? It's 1974 and he sees an ad saying "Drink Canada Dry". So he gets on a plane and does just that.'

Setting a half-sucked lollipop down beside his keyboard, the reporter to my left barks out a laugh that stops abruptly as he plugs the thing back in his mouth. A titter starts up behind me, from the direction of the subs, and runs like a Mexican wave the length of their desk.

'So they decide to cremate him . . .' comes a voice from the direction of Sport. 'It takes three weeks to put out the flames.'

Somewhere, a work experience embarks on the threadbare Miss World anecdote, its punch line ('Where did it all go wrong?') drowned out by groans of derision.

Next, cackles from Features and a rising refrain of, 'Go on, mate' prompt the picture editor to stand up and tighten an imaginary tie. ' "I've got good news and bad news," says the doctor to George Best. "The bad news is that you've only got an hour to live. The good news is that it's happy hour." '

For the first time since I heard the news of his death, two hours ago, I smile. George would have liked that one.

CHAPTER ONE

THE SUMMER OF 2003 – the George Best summer to me – was everything a great British summer should be. Those sharpened shadows on the bed sheets, the sunlight tickling your foot awake from beneath the blinds.

That Sunday in late July, the sun's lazy promise had a mocking quality. The three-year relationship that had lingered too long after university had ended two months earlier. There had been something poignant about the break-up, but nothing romantic about the regrets that continued to sneak up on me on good days and bad. Shaking off thoughts of him, I had pushed aside the sheets and stood at the open window with a glass of water, breathing in the stillness of the garden. It was the kind of stillness that was destined not to last.

It took my mobile phone, vibrating itself off the bedside table with a clatter, to shatter the early morning torpor.

'Celia?' My boss's voice brought a tightening in my gut. 'You've seen the papers, right?'

I always forgot. As a journalist, I was expected to leap out of bed at daybreak and plough my way through the national press. There was a pause as I failed to answer.

'It's entirely predictable, of course. I knew, we all fucking knew, that when we signed him up to do that column the whole thing would blow up in our faces. And now it's a right mess. I need someone out there to keep an eye on him.'

With no idea who he was talking about, I prayed for a clue.

'How bad is it?' I asked in a suitably world-weary tone.

'As bad as it gets. He's fallen off the wagon and Alex has left him again. He's currently in Malta drinking his way through Sliema, with reporters from every newspaper but ours in tow. It's only a matter of time before he decides to turn one of them into his boozing partner and gives them the exclusive he is contractually obliged to reserve for us. I need you on the next plane out.'

George Best. He was talking about George Best - the drunken, clapped-out, old footballer. Best had a ghostwritten, jauntily upbeat Sunday column in our paper reflecting his life after a controversial liver transplant. With little interest in footballers or alcoholics and still less curiosity for the travails of an alcoholic former footballer, I had never read it.

'You're far from ideal,' my boss was saying, 'you're too young and far too inexperienced – but his ghost, David, is in the States and right now you're the only one I can spare. We've booked you on a plane at midday and a room next to his at the Crowne Plaza. Pack, take a cab to Gatwick, find him, talk to him, get some idea of his mental state and for God's sake make sure he doesn't talk to any other reporters. Any questions?'

4

'How long will I be there?'

'Couple of days at most. We'll send a text confirming your travel arrangements and his agent's details – he will have warned George that you're on your way. When you do find him, don't let him out of your sight and whatever you do, don't have a drink with him, however persuasive he is. Keep your phone on at all times. We'll be calling in on the hour until you find him. And Celia? Take care.'

There is something appealing about being able to pack up and leave in less than an hour. But as I stared at the liquid sheen of the M25, the stirrings of excitement gave way to a mild panic. Other than the obvious, I knew nothing about George Best's life either before or since he stopped playing. I could do some Internet research at the other end, but for now, I needed a quick debrief. Andrew – my phone-a-friend who knows everything about everything – snorted derisively.

'Hardly a football nut, are you? Why are they sending you? I suppose they think he'll open up to a woman more easily. He likes his girls, Celia. A right playboy. Huge sex symbol. A few years back, you would have liked him.'

Andrew gave me the low-down on George's brief, astonishing career: his genius on the field, the first 'rock star' sportsman, the appeal to women, the whole cult of George Best – the 'Fifth Beatle'. He had touched the lives of everyone, it seemed, but me. This legendary status, followed by his long fall into disgrace, had kept people's appalled attention. Many felt they had a stake in his reconstruction.

By the time I was on the plane, I had read up on George. Here was a man who had been revered for his prowess on the field as well as for his personal charm and magnetic appeal. Even after his career faltered, the mercenary transfers to clubs such as the Los Angeles Aztecs and the Brisbane Lions did little to diminish his status. For some reason, we still loved him. What he endorsed, sold. We couldn't detach ourselves from his sex life and didn't think any less of him for steering clear of the troubled politics of his native Northern Ireland. Even his alcoholism, apparently, was lovable: his repeated attempts at recovery continued to evoke mass sympathy.

To date, my eighteen months as a journalist hadn't yielded much in the way of professional satisfaction. My time had largely been spent researching articles for my seniors, ambitions lulled by the gasp and wheeze of the photocopier. Once, a few months previously, I had been called into the feature editor's office and handed my first commission: interviewing a blind piano tuner who had regained her sight after falling down the stairs; the piece never made it into the paper. Now, faced with someone who gave every appearance of having been eviscerated by his own celebrity, and whose face – swollen by drink and self-indulgence – peered from the page on my lap into the camera as though attempting to find something lost there, I realised how easy it would be to fail. There was a logistical problem, for a start: how do you find someone who doesn't want to be found?

'I need you to babysit him,' my boss had said. 'If he won't talk, fine. Just don't let him talk to anyone else.'

I knew the term; I'd heard it used in scathing tones by reporters who rightly considered themselves above the menial role of shadowing a celebrity, whistleblower or politician's lover for days, sometimes weeks, in order to guarantee an exclusive or until their public value expired. The idea of babysitting George certainly wasn't beneath me, but I did wonder how, exactly, I would set about it. Surely it assumed a level of submission on his part? Something George, by the looks of things, would be unlikely to provide.

As the taxi drove me down a shoreline studded with fast food outlets, floodlights illuminating two watchtowers in the distance, I remembered my boss's final command: 'Call me tonight, as soon as you've found him. I want to know what kind of state he's in.' I wondered optimistically whether at this hour George might not simply be found in the hotel bar.

Pushing through the revolving doors into the marble-floored lobby of the Crowne Plaza, I realised immediately why this would be unlikely. The reception was blockaded by journalists posing as holidaymakers. There were a few exceptions: one couple, a grizzling baby in a pushchair at their feet, might be genuine. But the middle-aged Brit chatting to a member of staff by the lifts was certainly a hack, as were the groups of men on either side of me, wearing far too many clothes for the stifling temperature, hands clamped around their mobiles and their Marlboros. One voice, the brutal English diction jarring, as it so often does abroad, elevated itself above the others.

'Let's go through what we've got, yeah? Some good pictures of him by the pool, and Alex leaving for the airport – that's it at the mo ... And we have no idea where he's hiding out now – that's about the size of it ...'

Conscious, abruptly, of its volume, the voice suspended itself in mid-sentence. A sign – unseen by me – prompted the group to turn and give my clothing and hand luggage a suspicious once-over. There can't be many female holidaymakers in their early twenties who choose to stay at the Crowne Plaza alone. Silence gave way to an equally audible, hostile whisper: 'So? What do we reckon?'

'Don't know. Never seen her before.'

'Love?'

I had moved away, joining the queue at the front desk. But it was too late.

'Excuse me, love.'

The words, reiterated with emphasis, had every semblance of courtesy, but the face was devoid of sympathy.

'You got a light?'

'No, sorry, I don't smoke.'

'Good for you.'

There was a pause as, moving forward, I realigned myself with the queue.

'You here on holiday?'

'Yes.'

'Alone?'

'Yes.'

'Fair dos. Well you have a good time soaking up that sunshine.'

He was grinning now, having ascertained that I was, as he suspected, here for the same purpose as he was.

A knock on George's door yielded nothing, and I wandered out into the still-warm evening air. The streets of Sliema were thick with curdled smells and stag-nighters. Slighter, darker-skinned locals could be seen picking their way home with swift steps, past the cinnamon-scented churros sellers, eyes averted from a city which had long ago ceased to be their own. The surroundings, not picturesque enough to redeem themselves under its vulgar assault, did nothing to lift my spirits and I wondered why George would choose Sliema, out of anywhere in the world, as the place to heal an ailing marriage.

Using the biographical details I had read up on, I tried to calculate what George's frame of mind might be. Here was a man who had gone from the isolated, sectarian community of Northern Ireland to international stardom over the course of his formative years. A man whose fame had become unmanageable for him – as well as for his once teetotal mother, Ann, who had succumbed to alcoholism at forty-four. Things had degenerated still further after his mother's death, a decade later. Exactly a year ago, this same man had been given a new lease of life by a dangerous (and, if you believed the press, ill-deserved) liver transplant. Yet something had prompted him, along with everything invested in that revival, to self-combust. Within twelve months, the fifty-seven-year-old had started drinking heavily again and cheated on his wife.

If the newspaper clippings on the Internet were anything to go by, George's latest degeneration could be charted back to one night in early July. The former footballer had reportedly left his £1 million pound renovated barn in Lower Kingswood, Surrey, and headed straight to a nearby pub, The Chequers. There he'd ordered a glass of wine, and embarked on a week-long binge. Alex – the former Virgin airhostess left dead-eyed by her tumultuous eight-year marriage – had, at first, refused to forgive her husband this spree, packing her bags and posting the key to their home in a small, padded envelope to 'George Best c/o The Chequers'. But in an article dated two weeks ago (illustrated with a stoic-faced picture of Alex and the headline 'I'll Stand by My Man') she had declared that she was willing to give the marriage another try. George, apparently, didn't just fall off the wagon in style; he made up in style. A week after the relapse, Alex had awoken to find a BMW tied up with a pink ribbon in the driveway, two tickets to Malta tucked beneath the windscreen wiper. In one grandiose gesture, George had reclaimed his wife and his life.

The other woman had come as a complete surprise to both of them: Alex for obvious reasons; George because he couldn't remember her or, indeed, much of that lost week's carousing. Naturally, her claims had scotched any plans of reconciliation. I couldn't help but picture the scene: the two of them gradually breaking ground as they lounged by the pool by day and dined in local seaside restaurants by night, only to awake that Sunday to the front-page headline: 'George's Sly Kisses, Cuddles and a Dirty Weekend in London'.

In the clipping, Paula Shapland, a twenty-five-year-old, crop-haired taxi firm receptionist in indelible lip-liner, stared bolshily at the camera, trying in one muddied look to encapsulate both wronged woman and temptress. She would have been paid in the region of £10,000, I guessed, to describe their liaison with that breathless prudishness that characterises the kiss and tell. Describing the former foot-baller as 'relentless', she claimed to have been both 'flattered and shocked' by the 'seduction' which she had finally given in to in woodland behind George's local. Most lamentably for Alex, Paula's confessions included the allegation that suffering, perhaps, from pre-coital delusions, George had promised to divorce his wife and proposed a life of luxury by his side. She had left that woodland tryst rumpled but proud, her head filled with hazy notions of a new life as Mrs Best.

This verbal treachery had been the final straw for Alex: she had abdicated Malta, and the marriage, the night before.

'I've sent him packing,' she had tearfully told one reporter on arrival at Gatwick. 'I'm so hurt I can't stop crying, but I'm glad it's over. George is a very sick man and I've given him enough of my life. If he doesn't want to change, nobody can make him.'

Remembering the tension in my boss's voice, I saw this tangled knot of human failings from a newspaper's point of view: the whole shambolic scenario was manna.

Having scoured the fast food outlets and bars along the seafront fruitlessly, I climbed back up the hill into the old town, leaving behind the scrambled syncopation of the shore. There, I searched two brasserie-style restaurants – warmly lit with curled wooden pews – without finding any sign of George. My earlier pluck had given way to embarrassment, but I braved one last place, a casino where the screen idols lining the furry walls were pockmarked with condensation and the wooden furniture impregnated with grime.

'Excuse me, has ... has George Best been in here?'

My question provoked either mild amusement or a violent interest: 'Is he here? Why? Where is he staying?'

At the mere mention of his name, every man or woman of every nationality – even those far too young to have witnessed his heyday – reacted as though some precious pollen, impregnated with his greatness, had been released into the atmosphere. My father's attempt on the phone, earlier that day, to describe the colossal nature of his fame hadn't begun to approximate the reality. But, when a sunburnt Scot, slumped at the roulette table, repeated my question in three shades of incredulity to friends, encouraging them to 'Get a load of her', I decided to give up hope. George had been eluding journalists since before I was born – I had never stood a chance.

Throughout the two-hour search, my phone had whirred listlessly in my pocket – an answerphone message from the office I didn't have the courage either to listen to or delete. Back outside, pounding Maltese dance music safely reduced to an underwater beat, I looked at my watch: ten-fifteen. If I were an old Irish drunk, fleeing the paparazzi and craving a taste of home, where would I go? As I laughed to myself at the impossibility of that leap, the words of a friend of George's floated back to me from one of the cuttings: 'To him the pub is like his front room – that's one of the reasons he finds it so hard to stop drinking.'

'Do you speak English?' I shouted out to the humming local sweeping up broken glass outside a bar across the street. 'Do you know if there's an Irish pub in Sliema at all?'

Sucking a cut on his forefinger, he looked up at me. 'Irish, no; English, yes,' he replied in a heavy accent. 'You see the Crowne Plaza Hotel?'

I nodded.

'Behind it.'

I smiled. 'Thank you.'

The Lady Di was a sliver of a building, faux Tudor, squelched in between a corner shop and a derelict estate agent. Above its harlequin stained-glass windows, washing lines hung in great rumpled garlands the length of the street. I climbed three shallow steps and pushed open the door with trepidation. Aside from the barman, there were three people in the pub: two Maltese teenagers playing table football in the corner – and George.

Such was the potency of his image that I recognised him from his back alone. A slight, sullen figure, George sat on a stool at the bar, head bowed towards his wine in an attitude of semi-religious beatitude. Later, I understood that communion: it was the moment of release after the battle – that endless, lonely battle. It was the instant the inner torment was silenced. Back then, the man before me meant nothing more than a mission accomplished. I was relieved to have found him, yes, but disappointed too. This grey-haired old man in sun-bleached swimming shorts, wasted brown calves neatly crossed and surrender in the slope of his shoulders: this was George Best?

Laying down a plate of cheese and crackers before George without saying a word, the barman hovered, just in case the footballing legend two feet away decided to speak. I glanced at the boys in the corner, twisting and propelling their plastic figures back and forth: both appeared to be concentrating, but something in the tense angling of their bodies told me that they were aware of George's presence; that it was dictating every movement.

It took a few days with George, one of the most famous figures I am ever likely to meet, to understand that there were three kinds of reaction to fame. Those reluctant to defer to anything as vulgar as celebrity would put on a show of indifference until, weakened by a drink or two, resolve would be replaced by a craven sycophancy. Many of his older male fans were single-minded in their adulation, their sole desire being to discuss every goal George had ever scored, evoke every triumph, as though reliving those highlights in the presence of the man who had achieved them was the sharpest pleasure imaginable. And then there were the women. Less contrived in their approach, young or old, lower, middle or upper class, they would gravitate to him as if drawn by a force of nature. For them, his celebrity was all, and the belief that the gilt might rub off on them ran so deep that they would ignore any amount of rudeness or drunkenness. Paula Shapland's avid, opportunistic face; the trace of coquettishness in Alex's involuntary half-smile as she arrived home, genuinely broken, to be greeted by the country's paparazzi; George's celebrity had the capacity to rot everything close to it, puncture and deflate all that was real.

Dropping my bag down at my feet and slipping on to the stool beside him, I said quietly, 'George?'

CHAPTER TWO

H E DIDN'T LOOK UP.
    'George,' I tried again, faltering this time and unsure how to play my role. 'I've been sent by the paper to check up on you, make sure you're OK.'

Nothing.

I tried again. 'I'm the reporter your agent told you about. But I'm not here to bother you, just to help out any way I can.'

The barman, taking me for a fan, shot me an antagonistic look.

Remembering my boss's warning never to be seen drinking with him, and above all, never to buy him a drink, I sat on the next bar stool but one, ordered a Coke and sipped it slowly, conscious that George had hunched defensively over what I could see now was white wine spritzer – again, a disappointment, when I had expected vodka, whisky, a drunk of Richard Harris-like theatricality. Minutes passed as I waited for him to turn, out of politeness at least, towards me. He didn't.

'Can't you just leave me alone?' When he did speak, the words were spoken in one long exhalation.

Maybe it was the tiredness, or a sudden realisation of how absurdly my day had turned out, but rather than take offence, I began to laugh.

'Seriously,' he looked briefly at me, his eyes flashes of hostility, 'Will you just leave me alone – the lot of you?'

Marvelling at how familiar a face I had never set eyes on before could be, it took me a moment to answer. Those bristled eyebrows, the slack grey cheeks and dimples on his cheeks and chin were as instantly recognisable as fast food logos. And the scar, like the crease a sheet leaves on a face after a deep sleep, which ran above his left eyebrow – fifty-two stitches from a famous car accident a decade ago. Relevant or not, they were there, embedded in my psyche. But pictures hadn't done George's eyes justice: they were dimmed, I was sure, by drink, time and the adulation of others, but of such a light, vital blue that they seemed to conspire against the rest of his features to welcome and befriend. They had, with the sentimental language the famous tend to provoke, been described as 'dancing eyes', but time had stilled them, replacing their natural mirth with a wary arrogance. Around his nose and mouth, beneath a three-day stubble, the skin was parchment-thin, mapped with spidery blood vessels. And the lips – something happens to a person's mouth with celebrity: that narcissistic curl suggesting the erosion of any natural, instinctive responses.

'Did you hear me?' He had registered that I was still there. 'I'm asking nicely. Now can you please, please go away?'

It wasn't just that I was a journalist, I reasoned, taking in the freshly topped-up glass of wine on the bar; it was that I had interrupted a moment of ritualistic pleasure. People talk about enjoying a drink, but whether many of us have ever enjoyed one like George has is doubtful. Not for him was the base habit of the methylated spirits drinker. George, I came to understand, felt for alcohol what the glutton feels for food: it hijacked every one of his senses. More than once, during our subsequent time together, I would see his mouth fill with saliva at the prospect or memory of it, with a reaction as involuntary and primitive as a dog's. Then, when that bottle or glass arrived – a harmless social prop to most of us – he would finger the stem of it tenderly, with the sensual appreciation of the blind, postponing the pleasure for as long as he was able. That night, I began to understand the lifelong hold drink had over him. If he crossed to the other side of the room, separated from his drink for even a moment, I would catch him throwing fleeting glances in its direction, semi-regret, semi-anticipation, like two lovers separated by the crowd at a party. Drink, George later admitted to me, brought with it none of the jumble, none of the pressures or demands of human beings.

'Do you mind if I just sit here, George? If I promise not to say anything?' I was surprised to hear myself say the words out loud. 'It's taken me all night to find you.'

But I began to talk, because there was nothing else for it, because I hadn't had a conversation with anyone in six hours and was as unimpressed by him as he was by me. After a few minutes of ignoring my chatter, George's shoulder blades melted into the slouched green hump of his back. He turned, and we surveyed each other with mutual indifference.

'You said your piece?'

Picking up a piece of cheese, he examined it critically before replacing it on its cracker.

I had one shot at this. 'Look, I know that the last thing you want is for me to be here right now, but there must be at least thirty British journalists out here – all wanting the story. If I go back ...'

He held a hand up, shaking his head in disbelief. 'The story? I love the way you lot speak. The story, as you put it, is my life, the end of my marriage. And let me guess – I'm the villain here, right?'

'No,' I stammered, amazed that this was even in doubt, but aware also that on some level – perhaps because it was about him – George had begun to enjoy the conversation. 'Your column's one of the most read things in the newspaper. People look up to you: they want to believe the best. You should see the letters we get ...'

All of this was true, and having now read a dozen or so of his most recent columns, I could understand why. They weren't, as I'd imagined, about reliving a heyday which few beneath the age of forty could remember. They were the confessions of a flawed genius whose constant attempts to bring himself back from the brink drew the reader in. What brought them back in their millions, week after week, was the certainty that he would fail.

'They love me, but they want to tear me to shreds, right?'

I paused. I had wrongly assumed that guilt and self-blame would be the major part of this equation.

'Right,' I said hesitantly. 'But I – we – are not looking to tear you to shreds, George. You're one of ours. I'm here because we want to make sure that people know what you've been going through. But the truth of it, not the lies the others have been printing.' I doubted they were lies, but I seemed to be getting through to him. I cleared my throat. 'It's important that you use the paper to put forward your side of the story.'

It was easy, in the beginning, to sound convincing because I believed that I was protecting him from himself. Later, when the passive babysitting I had been assigned to do had turned into a more straightforward reporting job, and I would recount his drunken rants to the news desk, I became less sure. Still, that night, when I didn't yet know him, our relationship appeared uncomplicated to me and, mercifully, short-lived.

'Look, I'm not here to pester you,' I went on. 'We understand that this is a tough time for you. Actually,' I had a hunch this might amuse him, 'they call it "babysitting". Technically, all I'm here to do is mind you. And then at some point,' I ventured as casually as I could, taking another sip of Coke, 'if you were happy to, you and your ghost-writer could talk through some ideas for your next column.'

'You're here to *babysit* me?' His tone was different, softer than a leer but challenging and ironical. It was the first time he had addressed me in the way a man does a young girl, and I remembered the potted sexual past I had mugged up on: the estimated thousand women he'd slept with; the four – and not seven – Miss Worlds ('It was only four,' he used to joke. 'I didn't turn up for the other three.'). 'I'm a lucky man, aren't I? You look like you still need a babysitter yourself . . .'

'I'm older than I look,' I replied, succeeding only in sounding defensive, immature – and a little afraid, something I hadn't known I was until that moment. 'The main thing is that I'm on your side,' I persevered, anxious to reassert control. 'You're the paper's star columnist and they've promised to see you through this. So you can relax.'

And when he did, with a bitter laugh and a shake of the head, I was surprised to find that he was good company. Alert and quick-witted, arrogant but self-deprecating, George wasn't, as I had expected, a natural loner. In fact it was this innate sociability which had, by the time I met him, rendered his only two surviving states impossible. Abstinence meant giving up the very conviviality he drank for, while alcoholism was driving him deeper and deeper into loneliness.

I counted nine white wine spritzers that night, each one savoured slowly, not downed in one, as I had naïvely imagined. Eventually, one of the Maltese youths plucked up the courage to come over and ask for his autograph. Using the barman's pen, which skated about on the back of a flyer advertising a local gym, George obliged, but it had broken the sense of anonymity, and shortly afterwards he got up and began to shuffle towards the door.

'Hey,' I grabbed my jacket from the back of the chair and went after him. 'Wait for me. I thought we had an understanding.' I added a little laugh, to diffuse that last sentence of its imperiousness. He stopped outside the pub, a single streetlight waxing his complexion.

'An understanding? Piss off. Do whatever you like – I'm going back to my hotel.'

Following at a discreet distance, I took in the slight shoulders and torso that dwindled into fragile legs, like the top-heavy doodles of a child. At my age, these legs had brought him great glory; now – though he was younger than my father – he looked like a dead man walking.

'I've found him,' I whispered into my phone triumphantly. 'He's right here. What should I do?'

'What kind of a state is he in?'

I looked up at George's unapologetic back, the scored white lines across his sunburnt neck.

'It's hard to tell. Drunk, obviously, but not as out of control as I'd thought he'd be. He's heading back to the hotel now, so hopefully he'll go straight to bed.'

'Right,' my boss sounded sceptical. 'Stay with him, OK? Do not let him out of your sight for a second. Have you seen any other journalists?'

I snorted. 'Yes – the hotel's crawling with them.'

I heard the tension in his breath rise a notch.

'Has he spoken to any of them?'

'No. I double-checked – and he was tricky enough with me, so we're safe there.'

'Thank God for that. Still, you could be in for a long night, I'm afraid. If people ask you, try and fudge the journalist thing, will you? Say you're a friend or a PA or something. Nobody knows you,' he added, more to himself than me, 'so it should be fine. But when he's ready to turn in, I want you to escort him right back to his hotel room and pull the door shut behind him, OK? I'm counting on you. Don't mess this up.'

I wasn't listening. George had pushed through the hotel's revolving doors and was heading left to the bar where four of the journalists I had spotted in the lobby earlier were playing pool.

'Celia?'

'Yes.'

'Remember what I said: you are not at any point to pay for his drink or have one with him, OK? You can drink the whole minibar dry once you're back in your room, I don't give a damn, but remember what I said: do not be seen boozing with him. It would compromise the paper, right?'

With that, he hung up.

Jovial, wincingly insincere cries of 'George' greeted Best's entrance to the reception. Joining him at the bar, I touched his elbow gently.

'George, listen, it's late, why don't we just call it a night and go to bed?'

Raising an eyebrow, he leaned in so close that I could make out the black and white sprinkle of his stubble, the odd russet shoot pushing through, smell the tartness of his breath – and a base note of something sour that his pores seemed to secrete.

'I'm not sure I'm that kind of man.' He pushed his mouth out into an absurd moue and cocked his head to one side. 'You young girls are pretty direct these days, aren't you?'

Catching the exchange, one of the journalists broke into a mocking laugh.

'George, come on. You gonna be bossed about by a girl?' He put a hand theatrically to his chest. 'You're breaking my heart, mate. Come and have a drink with us.'

'Yeah, George, come on,' heckled another. 'We've just bought a bottle of champers.'

Enjoying his audience, George began to smile. It was a demonic smile, setting off that dimpled little boy look, in which the sweetness had fermented into something cruel.

'George . . .'

But he was already holding out a champagne glass to be filled, and I had no choice but to join him at their table and perch, as casually as I could, on a nearby stool. If confidences did start being exchanged, what was I to do – reach out and gag him?

'His minder, are you?'

The taller of the two journalists was trying to distract me, while the other began to quiz George about Alex, asking him whether his marriage was over.

'No,' I stammered. 'I'm just keeping an eye out for him – that's all.'

'Sure you are.' The journalist turned to George, 'So, do you and your friend fancy a game of pool?'

'She's here to babysit me,' George slurred.

'Is she now?' the two journalists smiled at one another.

'I mean do I look like a baby to you? Do I?' Pushing down on his knees, he raised himself with some effort. 'Let's have that game then.'

'OK,' I stood up.

George looked scornfully in my direction. 'Girls can't play pool.'

'Oh yes they can.' My bravado rang false, but it was the only way to stay with him.

An hour later, we were on our third game, and my vision was skewed with tiredness. George, to my relief, had become taciturn and monosyllabic, eyes overlaid with a vitreous film nothing could permeate. By now every journalist in the bar had seized any opportunity they could to casually question him, but their efforts – apart from one aborted outburst about Alex – were largely wasted.

'George,' I whispered in his ear, 'let's head off, eh?'

Surprised by the meekness of his response, I escorted him out of the bar. Once in the lift, George perked up, while I sank down, hollow-limbed, on the banquette.

'You could come back to my room, for a nightcap, you know . . .' He said it without conviction, as a matter of course.

I couldn't help but smile. 'So this is the charm they talk about. No, I don't think so, George.' A pause. 'Aren't you knackered? I am.'

'Fair enough.' Unused to being rebuffed, he attempted a smile, his brows sinking into a frown, eyes reduced to shadowy hollows in the electric orange light.

We were outside his room now. Following my boss's instructions, I waited as he fumbled with the plastic keycard, knowing I was only free to go once I'd seen that door shut behind him.

'You're sure you won't come in?' The lightness in his tone was gone, his expression anything but inviting now. 'Last time I'll ask.'

'George, I'm . . .'

Before I'd had a chance to finish he had pushed me clumsily against the doorframe, threading a knee between my legs. When I tried to move my head to one side, he gripped my jaw with his right hand and advanced a grim face towards mine.

'Christ, George,' I disengaged myself with a jolt and he slumped against the doorframe. 'What are you playing at?'

I wasn't scared — he was too far gone to be threatening – but the brush of stubble and tang of his breath snapped whatever it was that had kept me strong all day. I wondered, wearied by the thought, whether this was what it was going to be like between us: him lunging, me fending him off.

'George, you need to get some sleep. We both do.' The

door slammed shut in response, and I paused a moment before calling out, 'Tell me if you need anything, won't you? I'm right next door.'

An hour later, roused from an instant, dreamless sleep by the clean smack of a palm against my door, I regretted those words.

'Let me in ...'

Recognising the whimper as belonging to George, I put my eye to the spy hole. Clad in one of the hotel's white towelling dressing gowns, his features magnified into a grotesque caricature, he stared through the door with such intensity that I felt sure he could see me. He must have drunk more since I'd left him, I realised as I climbed back into bed, and I resolved to confiscate the key to his minibar the next morning.

For the second day running, I awoke to my boss's voice. The conviction that, on some very basic level, this was wrong, coupled with the bleary realisation that the alarm clock had failed to go off, hit me in quick succession.

'Well, that's just great, isn't it.'

I wasn't sure whether it was a question.

'Morning – what's going on?'

'What's going on is that somehow George has managed to give a full interview to another paper in which he claims to have enjoyed a recent threesome.' I heard the angry rustling of a paper. '"I'm not in love with my wife any more and I want to drink – it's got nothing to do with anyone else."'

'Don't,' I managed feebly. 'Please. He swore to me that he hadn't spoken to a soul since Alex left. I honestly don't know how that happened ... It must have been the night before I got here.'

George's early morning visit floated back to me, with the nebulous quality of a bad dream. Had he been going to warn me? 'Let me speak to him and call you back.'

'Don't bother calling back,' my boss snapped. 'Just stick to him like glue from now on, and find out if he's blabbed to anyone else, right? Oh, and until we're able to get his ghost-writer to talk to him, you can at least try to find out what his immediate plans are. Keep us ahead of the game.'

I lay immobile for a moment. What was I doing here? Top British football managers had failed to keep George in order and in the short space of time that I had known him, he had already lied to me with a chilling ease. The only thing this job was likely to prove was that I was too green for a challenge like this one.

Remembering that I'd ordered all the English papers when I checked in the night before, I opened my door to find them there, hanging ponderously from my doorknob in a raffia bag. Whatever I'd expected, it was worse: gory details about the state of his marriage, health and unaffected sexual prowess were laid out in all their squalid splendour on pages 2, 3 and 4.

I showered, dressed and knocked on George's door, feeling murderous. My first lesson, learned the previous night, had been about my charge's relationship with alcohol. That morning I learned my second: that it was impossible to stay angry with George for long. Though out of keeping with an alcoholic's temperament, a Pavlovian optimism was his default mood, so that no matter what atrocities he had committed the night before, he was always sweetly upbeat in the mornings. Today, he seemed to believe, was the start of a brand-new life.

This went some way to explain why, despite his eventful night, George opened the door looking fresh and alert, the earnestness of his smile forcing me to swallow the recriminations rising in my throat.

'How's my sitter?'

A piece of fluff from the hotel towel, caught in the bristle of his stubble, grated like a deliberate ploy to disarm, and I checked the impulse to brush it off.

'Not so good, George.' I paused, uncomfortable at the intimacy of our surroundings. 'Why didn't you tell me that you'd spoken to that reporter the night before I got here? You said that you'd kept well clear of any journalists. After everything we discussed, couldn't you at least have warned me?'

'Oh, you mean Kate?'

I shrugged. 'Whoever, George – yes, Kate.'

I looked for some twitch of contrition or apology in his face, just as I had the day before when we were discussing Alex, but found nothing.

'Did she tell you?'

I couldn't believe it; he was smiling.

'Pretty little thing, isn't she? Anyway she turns up here, bold as brass, with a bottle of champagne. I let her in 'cause I quite fancied a little nightcap ... Oh, and would you believe it?'

The vanity in his expression, unchecked, was embarrassing. I had often wondered whether fame – because of the sexual possibilities it afforded – corrupted men more deeply than it did women. Here was proof. But there was something else: it was (I suspected then, and found out for sure

27

later) all fibs. The champagne and the visit were no doubt at his suggestion. But after years of being lusted after, George couldn't understand that the days of women not having an ulterior motive were gone.

'She was all over me. The woman was all over me, but I didn't sleep with her. We had a drink, a chat.' He examined me for a reaction. 'A kiss and a fumble, and then she left. Did you see her downstairs this morning?' He winked. 'Have a girly chat?'

I laid the paper silently down on the bed.

'That little b—' he began to stammer, picking it up. 'She'd said she ...' Any residual anger evaporated before George's genuine bafflement and the surprising discovery that, sober, he was reluctant to swear in front of me. 'She said it was all off the record; said she was my number one fan ...' Aware now how gullible he sounded, he peered up at me, the gurgling source of a laugh in his throat. 'I never said any of this.'

I didn't yet know him, but I was convinced he was lying.

'But you think it's funny?'

'Not really – the stuff about Alex isn't going to help. Not that things with my lovely wife could be made much worse.' He paused. 'I used to enjoy getting drunk and reading about what I'd done in the papers. You could relive the fun of it all, you know? But then people started just making stuff up, taking me for a fool just because I was drunk.' His face darkened. 'That I don't like.'

Pushing swollen ankles – branches of veins straining up against their purplish brown surface – into the cushioned mouths of his trainers, he began to lace them silently, throwing the occasional, now sheepish, glance, my way. I felt a bubble of dislike for this wreck of a man rise in my throat and burst into nothing.

'Look, I'm sorry about that girl. Got you into trouble, did I? Or are we a bit jealous?' he added, with what he imagined was a rakish smile.

I couldn't help but laugh at the absurdity of the situation, and the lack of correlation between the way George saw himself and the poignant reality – but also with relief. My charge was as spoilt and vainglorious as my research had suggested he might be – but there was a humour and self-awareness there that would make the job bearable. And I felt that he was getting used to me too: the testy manner of the night before had been replaced by a natural warmth, as if he were caught between tolerating my presence and enjoying it. Again it occurred to me that he was not a man who liked to be alone for long.

'Have you had anything to eat?' he grinned, relieved too that his misdemeanours seemed to have been forgotten. 'Fancy having breakfast with George Best?'

'George?'

'Yes?'

'I can't believe you just referred to yourself in the third person.'

The restaurant was a high-ceilinged affair with a vicious air-conditioning system and walls the colour of tinned mushrooms. I spotted a posse of journalists immediately, loading themselves up with fried breakfasts, pausing only to register George's arrival, and guided him to the table furthest away, overlooking the pool.

'What's in the bag?' I asked.

He had set it down on the chair beside him: a Sainsbury's carrier bag I recognised from the right before.

'My sweeties; my pills. There are quite a lot of them.'

He opened the plastic bag wide for me to see. There were packets of them, labels dense with directions and precautions, while others – blue, green, purple and white – were jumbled loosely in amongst their sets of crumpled instructions.

I lowered my voice. 'What do they all do?'

'Well, the important ones, the Antabuse tablets, have been sewn into my stomach lining. I know: weird, right? But those green ones there? They're for my new liver, the pink ones are for the depression caused by the green ones – and so it goes on.'

'But last night, George – how could you drink that much, with the Antabuse pellets in your stomach, I mean?'

He drew himself up tall with mock pride. 'Well, you may not know this, but I have something of a history with alcohol.'

'You do?'

'Oh yes,' he replied, deadpan. 'So they don't quite incapacitate me as they should, which really amazed the doctors, I can tell you. That said, they do make me throw up, oh, every ten minutes or so. Not great. You might've noticed me going to the toilet quite a bit last night.'

I had, but had thought nothing of it.

'Yeah,' his surface expression was jokey now; the one beneath it unreadable. 'That, I'm afraid, is my punishment. Right,' he opened the menu with a flourish, 'what are we having?'

I asked for toast and jam; he ordered Coco Pops.

'Coco Pops?' I repeated when the waiter had left.

'Love them,' he said, helping me, then himself, to some tea. 'My mum never had sweets in the house when I was a child; now you're allowed them for breakfast. Coco Pops and Frosties,' he added guilelessly, stirring half a sugar cube into his cup. 'I can't get enough of them.'

My notion that alcoholics were not interested in food was discarded, along with the other preconceptions — the preference for hard liquor, cranky mornings and dull conversation.

Being deprived of sweets and chocolate when he was growing up was only one reason for George's sweet tooth. Alcohol, I found out later, caused his blood sugar levels to fluctuate dramatically, which meant that during the brief periods when George wasn't drinking, he would hoover up Snickers bars and Jelly Babies with the hungerless greed of a young boy, shedding their wrappers in his wake.

We ate in silence, thinking our separate thoughts as we gazed at the mothers and children setting up their paraphernalia near the shallow end of the pool.

'How do you not get upset, George, when someone betrays you like that girl did?'

I doubted she had 'betrayed' him (George was a lot of things, but not naïve), still, I was intrigued to know how much journalists had the power, if at all, to permeate his world.

Chewing on a piece of my toast, he pondered.

'I guess it still upsets me,' he said finally. 'People think that you don't feel things when you become well-known. Of course you do, but it doesn't linger, and it doesn't ...' He stirred half a spoonful of sugar into his fresh tea. 'I suppose it doesn't matter like it used to. When I started out, you lot decided I was God. I remember first seeing the word "godlike" written in a paper about me. I didn't know how to handle it at all – how could I?' He rubbed hard with his knuckles at the stubble that was a day or two away from becoming a beard, lowering his eyes so that I could make out the leafy blue stencils on his lids. 'But when the press decided to turn against me, that – the quickness of the change, I mean – that I did have trouble with.'

There was no real equivalent to the fickle nature of the media in life, he explained, and I was surprised by the meditative nature of his tone. Even in personal relationships, he pointed out with reason, you never saw the same about turn, from worship to the desire to smash that person up.

'Celebrities,' he perfected a mock bow at the table, 'like myself, will tell you they always hated the press. That's just not true. When they're nice about you, when all you read is compliments, people comparing you to a Beatle, to a film star you grew up idolising ...' he looked up at the ceiling and I let him wallow, for a minute, in the memories. 'That feels so good that you start to depend on it, you know? Start to forget the other things you have going for you. I was just a boy when I left Belfast to join Manchester United, and praise from you lot,' he gestured smilingly at me with his chin, 'pretty quickly took the place of my own parents' approval.' He shook his head. 'That front page became a barometer of how well I was doing – and not just on the pitch. Then what happens is that you start to perform for them, provoke them, you know, like a kid.'

He began to laugh: an Irish laugh which seemed to find the humour even in sad things, and I wondered why he was talking in the past tense, as if he weren't still performing and provoking 'us lot' now.

'It got worse and worse, the stuff they would say about me. Once,' his eyes widened, 'years ago, a piece appeared saying that I'd had underage sex with a girl.'

It was strange, sitting across the breakfast table from a man and having no idea whether something that would damn him so completely was true or not. Like everyone, I had caught friends or acquaintances telling me white lies over the years, observed with interest the twitching foot beneath the table and inability to keep eye contact, reassured by the notion that if you look closely enough it's possible to guess whether a person is telling the truth. Looking at George now told me nothing. Was he capable of having underage sex with a girl? From the fragments of character I had assembled in the past twenty-four hours, anything was possible.

'She was a child,' he was looking beyond me, beyond the journalists sticking it out at their tables, their breakfasts long ago finished. 'The whole thing was made up, of course, so I sued the paper for a hundred grand and they settled out of court. Now,' he flicked back an imaginary quiff in a gesture of insouciance, 'there's not much left that either hurts or surprises me any more, which is a blessing, I suppose.'

After breakfast George made no objection to me joining him by the pool, making salacious jokes about the bikini he hoped I'd be wearing and the gossip we might fuel, but it was clear that something had tainted his mood. Was he annoyed with himself for having been honest with me – or was that candour part of his shtick? It was hard to tell.

We'd settled on neighbouring sunloungers at a discreet corner of the pool. I'd wanted to revive our earlier banter, but he'd promptly pulled a thriller from his bag.

'I didn't have you down as a bookworm,' I said without thinking.

'Why?' he asked, using his hand as a sun visor. 'Because I'm famous?'

I thought about it, lining up my preconceptions about celebrities. My assumption was that they were mostly damaged philanderers who, because of an all-consuming narcissism, were incapable of non-self-serving interests. The characters you read about in newspapers and magazines tended to confirm this, while those challenging this conviction weren't, by definition, widely written about.

'Yeah – maybe.' I observed him for signs of offence and found none. 'You want to know what a lot of people think? That famous people just sit around being famous.'

'And some of them do,' he nodded, retrieving a pair of Raybans from his back pocket. 'It's a full-time job, isn't it? But I wonder ... Do you really think that because I'm a footballer, I'm thick?'

I noted the present tense.

'First of all, I never said *thick* – that was your word, and not what I meant at all. And second of all, I know nothing about football, as you've probably guessed, so the lot of you could be Einsteins ... Are you?'

He fell silent, and I couldn't read the expression behind his glasses.

'I think it's fair to say that sportsmen aren't always the sharpest knives in the drawer,' he said eventually. 'People liked to say that it was me who would make those jokes about Gazza ...'

'Which jokes?'

'You know: me telling him that his IQ was less than the

number on his shirt, and then him asking, "What's an IQ?" That sort of thing.'

I laughed. Having initially drawn parallels between George and Gascoigne – whose descent into alcoholism and depression was charted weekly in the news – I was intrigued to know what their relationship was.

'Are you two friends?'

'I've always had a lot of respect for him.' His tone had changed: this wasn't something he wanted to discuss. 'But people like to describe us in the same sentence, when in fact we're two different people who both happen to play football and have problems.'

I wanted to probe more deeply, but George was back to the point he was making.

'So look: I've met some very clever players (and some damned stupid journalists, incidentally), but I guess it's true that some of the lads really do have their brains in their feet, hands or wherever. Then again, what use is being clever to them, really?'

'What do you mean?'

'Well, I would use books to escape on long coach journeys or fill in the time at hotels, but do you think anyone's really going to care what I think? I can have a conversation about anything you like, but people only ever want to talk to me about football.'

I wondered, fleetingly, whether that thwarted intelligence had anything to do with his alcoholism; whether he felt guilty about the one natural gift – obscured by his looks and talents on the pitch – that he had never made full use of.

'I suppose I didn't think you'd be someone who finds it easy to relax either.'

35

Putting his book down he looked across at me with an amused expression.

'All these ideas you have about me – where do they come from? I'd got the distinct impression – and correct me if I'm wrong here – that you haven't exactly followed my career trajectory . . .'

'Maybe not, but I've done my research.'

'Your research?' His laughter put me at ease, gave me the reassuring sense that we were building something, talking like this. 'My problem is that relaxing means one thing to me, but I do like reading. I wasn't great at school, but I always got good marks in English and Mensa tell me I've got an IQ of 158.' I smiled at the detail. 'You, on the other hand, don't find it easy to relax, do you?'

'What do you base that on?'

'No book – not even a girly magazine – no suntan cream, and a full set of clothing.'

He gestured at the T-shirt and jeans shorts I was still wearing, and I looked down at the denim sticking to my thighs, and wondered what was making me too self-conscious to take them off.

'Is it me, or is it your colleagues,' he gestured at a group of young men settling directly opposite us on the other side of the pool, 'that's making you so shy?'

For an old drunk, he noticed things.

'Honestly? I'm not sure. I'm here to work, you know, so . . .'

'Bet you were a regular little head girl at school. Or were you busy chasing boys?'

I swatted a fly off my foot.

'Neither really . . .'

'So why are you lying there, fully clothed, in the baking sun? Get into your swimsuit and enjoy the weather.'

'I was going to but now you've built it up too much,' I smirked. 'Anyway, I'm going to go and get us some iced water in a minute,' I lied.

'Bollocks,' he said, closing his eyes. 'You're worried about what the other journos will think. Or you think I might pounce when I see the wonders you're hiding under that lot. Then again, there's always the third possibility: that you're covered in thick, black hair. Which one is it?'

Resigned, I pulled off my T-shirt and shorts, as he took it all in through one lizard-like eye. He was right about the other journalists; increasingly hard to recognise in their semi-nudity, I was sure they were everywhere. Meanwhile, with the tape in my Dictaphone still blank, I had nothing to tell the office.

'You can do my back if you like,' came George's stifled murmur from his prone position on the lounger.

'Can I? Thanks, George.'

I heard him smile.

'Well if you're going to babysit you may as well make yourself useful.'

The skin was still taut across his shoulders, pulled tightly across the narrow, muscled width of his frame, but lower down, towards his back, where the flesh was more feminine, it had begun to slacken and jaundice in the manner of a man some two decades older. Having feared I might find the act repugnant after last night's lunge – this morning, he appeared to be a different person – I was relieved to feel just a slight awkwardness, a consciousness that the movements should be brisk and businesslike.

37

'Not too high a factor, is it? I don't usually wear cream and I want a good tan – this is the start of the fight-back,' he whispered, his voice slack with sleep. 'I'm telling you . . .'

I wiped my hands on a towel and lay back. Now might be a good time to call the office, plan our next move.

Just under an hour later, I awoke to find George on his feet, sinews clenched.

'What the . . . ? Look at that!' I followed his trembling finger in the direction of a faceless woman on the other side of the pool, hidden behind her copy of the *Daily Mirror*. George was on the cover, mouth open in a battle cry, presumably hurling abuse at the photographer. 'Best Loses It' read the headline.

'Oh, yes.'

I hadn't shown him that one, it being more of a picture story than anything else.

'I've had enough of this – do I look like I'm losing it to you? Do I?'

'We've known each other for less than twenty-four hours, George,' I joked, conscious now that humour could diffuse his rages, and wondering whether I might be able to turn this outburst to my advantage. 'And right now, you do look like you're losing it. Sit down.'

He did.

'Look,' I baited, lowering my voice. 'You were right about people wanting to tear you down.'

'They want to, but they won't,' he muttered, settling back down with a shaking jaw. 'What am I? A national sport or something? And as for that girl who set me up for the papers . . .'

I looked around. Most of the tourists had disappeared for

lunch, but the journalists were still there. Aside from the shrieks of delight and dismay from toddlers in the shallows, the pool area had descended into a sun-induced torpor; that Irish accent would carry.

'I don't like to call that Paula woman what she really is,' he went on, adopting the moralistic tone he had used to describe the female journalist who had come to his hotel room, 'because I have always been one to respect women, and I've dealt with a fair few of them in my time who were a lot brassier than she was, I can tell you.' He turned a hard face towards me. 'But she wasn't a lady.'

Not much respect there, then.

'These women nowadays,' he leaned forward, impassioned, 'they're something else.'

'All of them, George?' I couldn't help myself. 'Are women really worse behaved around celebrities than they were forty years ago, in the swinging sixties and seventies?'

'Miles worse. You should see these girls: they come and talk to me or knock on my hotel room door and ask if they can come in, only it's not like it was before because they always end up squealing. That cow in my local was hired by the press to set me up, I know she was, and she'll get her comeuppance.'

There he was, through some warped sense of gentlemanly courtesy, holding back on the word 'bitch' again, yet his sentences were packed with equally misogynistic references. I had thought, only a few hours earlier, that there was something touching, untainted, about his adoration of women, but perhaps that too had soured.

'There are people I know, in London,' he was saying,

'who could sort that girl out. They've done it before when I've been double-crossed.'

Both curious and embarrassed by these sub-Mafioso threats, I turned towards him. 'What are you going to do, George? Have Paula beaten up?' He threw me a loaded look and I turned away. 'Well, I'm not sure how seriously I can take you with that smear of sun cream on the side of your nose.'

For a moment I thought I'd gone too far, half-expecting him to tell me to piss off again – or get up and walk away. But a second passed, and he broke into a crooked smile.

'Have you been letting me go on all this time?' He was laughing gruffly now, rubbing a nostril ineffectively.

'Here.' Reaching over and wiping off the dash of white with a corner of a towel, I goaded, 'You were saying, Don Corleone.'

'You got it with you?'

'What?'

Laying his head back down, he closed his eyes. 'Your pad and pencil, your tape recorder – whatever it is you guys use nowadays.'

'Of course. I just need to give the office an update on how you're feeling, and what your plans are now.'

'Right.'

Taking a long slug from the water bottle beside him and shooting a quick glance at the tape recorder on the white plastic table between us, he began. 'It was all supposed to be going so well. "My rehabilitation" they kept calling it, as though because I had had the op, and because I had a new liver, my head would change too. Alex was over the moon. She had all these plans.'

He barked out a laugh filled with rancour – a laugh that didn't need to be theatrical but was. Force of habit, maybe.

'We were going to start afresh, and I was going to seal the deal on a couple of pretty lucrative endorsements which would mean endless exotic holidays of the kind she loves – Jesus, you should see the money these guys offer just to stick your face on a packet or use your name and get a few snaps of Alex in a bikini. And these were all things I couldn't do before, when I was drinking. Only . . .' he ran age-dappled, oddly refined fingers down from his cheek-bones to his chin, 'only it turns out that I didn't feel much like celebrating or doing anything much. Turns out I actually felt pretty crap.'

'It must have been a lot of pressure,' I attempted, in the therapy speak we journalists use to lull our subjects into a confessional frame of mind. 'Feeling that everyone was watching you – and that you'd been given this incredible chance.' It was possible to goad and feel sympathetic at the same time, but I didn't, couldn't yet feel any sympathy for this man I hardly knew.

'Yep,' he paused, looking away. 'That, and the fact that I felt weak, physically. Then one day Alex and I had this stupid fight, the kind of fight people have all the time. I can't even remember what it was about.' With a moan, he had it: 'The dogs, that's what it was. Anyway, I stormed out of the house, not knowing where I was going – honestly. And I found myself driving past The Chequers – my local. As I got nearer,' his hand, curled redundantly on his chest, gave an involuntary spasm, 'it was like somebody else took over, like I was sleepwalking but at the same time totally conscious of what I was doing. I remember thinking, *I remember thinking*, "I'll only be a minute" and I went in and ordered a spritzer. Just like that.'

Out of nowhere a four-year-old in oversized shorts materialised with a piece of paper and a pencil.

'Of course I'll sign it for your mum.' Handing the paper back and ruffling the boy's hair distractedly, he went on. 'Only at first, the landlord, who's fairly new there, tells me that he can't serve me.' His listless eyes stopped moving along the rows of prone poolside figures and met mine. 'The local lot like to look after me; they call themselves the Press Gang, always fending off reporters, giving me lifts and so on. The landlord's a great bloke too, but you don't want great blokes around when all you're after is a bloody drink. Well, I didn't want to cause a scene, so I pretended I was joking, asked for a fruit juice instead, and went outside into the beer garden. It was then that some blonde, a fan – my "number one fan" actually; they're never just "a fan" – who'd been at the bar earlier came up. She'd seen the whole thing happen; thought it was a scandal. "It's a free country," she says. And she puts a glass of white wine down in front of me.'

As he told the story, something funny was happening to George. His body had been beset by a multitude of tics: bouts of frenzied leg scratching were alternated with the raking of teeth over the scale of dry skin lining his bottom lip. 'Actually, she wasn't my type at all,' he went on, 'sort of boyish and flat-chested, but when she started sitting on my knee, complaining she felt cold, and I'd had a few . . .'

A suppressed anguish was gaining on him and I wondered whether this was the remorse I had expected to find the night before.

'Well, the rest is pretty foggy, but I am sure of two things: I didn't sleep with her and the whole thing,' he jabbed a finger at me, 'was a set-up if ever I saw one.'

He sat up abruptly and began to pull his trainers on.

'I think that's me done. It's hot and I'm not meant to be in direct sunlight too long, you know, because of the pills. I'm like a gremlin,' he pulled a face. 'That's what they've reduced me to.'

That was it? That was all he was prepared to give me? Only then did I understand: the talk of alcohol had done it. And right now George had to have a drink.

'Well, look,' I was up in an instant, trotting behind him the length of the pool, 'let me come inside with you and cool down.'

Remembering that I wasn't dressed, I jogged back over to the lounger. A middle-aged woman in a floral swimsuit intercepted me.

'Excuse me, love!' I looked impatiently past her at George, disappearing inside the revolving doors of the hotel. 'You a friend of George's?' The use of his first name annoyed me; I wasn't sure why.

'Yes.' I smiled tightly.

'Terrible what's happened with him and Alex. We were only saying a couple of days ago, weren't we, Terry?' she shouted over at a reddening body some way off. 'That they were like a couple of honeymooners. I blame the press: persecuted they were, absolutely persecuted.'

'I couldn't agree more,' I smiled, taking in the copy of the *Sun* lying beside her. 'Sorry – I've got to dash.'

★   ★   ★

'You should have said there was a game on.'

Even to me, my tone sounded fraudulent. I didn't want to be there any more than he wanted me to be, but this job meant the denial of that most basic impulse – one probably felt more keenly by women than men – never to outstay your welcome. White wine spritzer in hand, he twisted a fraction on his bar stool so that he was facing the TV square on, blocking off any further conversation.

'That's right.'

'Who's playing?'

'Know something about football, do you?'

'Not a thing. I told you that. But I . . .'

'So why bother asking?'

It was strange to watch the change in him, the sudden hostility towards me, the same person he had been chatting to quite casually only moments ago. *In the grip*, I thought to myself, and the words made sense for the first time. I had never met anyone suffering from alcoholism before, yet it occurred to me now that it was misleading to call it a disease – it seemed to take away the weight of that inner conflict, somehow.

Over the time I subsequently spent with George, I learned to recognise the hunted look he would take on when the idea or association, however tangential, of alcohol seeded itself. Sometimes, as I had just witnessed, it would surprise even him with its vehemence. He could be in the middle of an anecdote, a book or a meal and his mind would slam shut. All courtesies and emotions would follow suit: closed to all but drink.

Lifting a second glass of white wine to his mouth and letting his eyes flicker shut for a millisecond, George took a small sip. The pleasure he was experiencing was so unchecked that – feeling like I had caught someone in a masturbatory act – I turned away. It seemed obscene for an addiction as raw as his to be indulged publicly, and in the same room where honeymooners were drinking mimosas. A few minutes passed, during which time I could feel the pigment seeping back into his world, one which, only a minute ago by the pool, must have seemed ashen.

Eyes still on the screen, an apology implicit, he asked, 'Would you like a drink?'

By the time I came back from the bar with an orange juice, George had made a decision.

'I'd like to add something to what I said before. I think you're right about putting the record straight. And this is not about that stupid tart. As if I'd get mixed up with some tramp like that. What, me? Why the hell would I?'

Astonished by an arrogance growing with every drink, I asked: 'So, what then?'

He exhaled slowly, and I knew that if not the truth, I would at least get an elaborate version of it that might appease the office.

'To be honest, things with Alex hadn't been good even before I started drinking again,' he began. 'The transplant, well, it made me so ill that I could barely walk, let alone . . .' Curling up the underside of his lip, valentine pink where the alcohol had gnawed through it, he shot me a prurient look. 'And before that I was drinking, wasn't I? So she was sort of,' he made an effort, 'bearing with me, being my nurse, which does kind of take the excitement out of a marriage. "Life is filled with compromise and scars." Who said that? Well, whoever it was was right, and for one hell of a long time, Alex was on the receiving end of both of those things.'

I pulled together everything I knew about Alex in my head, trying to imagine what this woman must have endured, and wondered, along with everyone else, why she had put up with him for so long. The magnitude of George's fame meant that I found it hard to sympathise as I should have, assuming that a pragmatic trade-off, spoken or unspoken, would have defined the marriage from the start. Couples who live out their relationships in public make it impossible for us to imagine that the mundanities and mid-level emotions which are the stuff of everyday life exist for them too, once the curtain has come down. I'd seen the paparazzi shots of Alex shopping, attending premières and posing for photo shoots in glossy magazines – living the dream and smiling, always, gracious enough to be conscious of the fact – but what was her relationship with George made up of the rest of the time? How much genuine affection was there underneath the PR gloss – and, besides, wasn't it possible for the two to co-exist?

Alex had been a twenty-two-year-old from Cheam in Surrey when she had first met George, then a forty-eight-year-old divorcee with one son. The obvious star-gazing and gold-digging accusations had been flung about by the press at the time. Feasting on the twenty-six-year age gap, everyone chose to disregard the fact that George was bankrupt, reduced to selling off his football trophies to keep himself afloat. Although none of it had stuck, a mistrust of Alex had persevered in the public's mind. A classmate of hers had told the press that she remembers the once fair-skinned school-girl saying, 'When I grow up I want to marry someone famous.' But so had most of the girls I had been at school with. And besides, George was already an alcoholic – albeit a more socially acceptable one – when the pair first met, so on every account hardly a fantasy prospective husband.

By today's standards their courtship had been discreet. Neither the engagement nor the marriage itself, at Chelsea Register Office, had been sold off to a glossy magazine as the orgy of spray-tanned flesh now known as a 'wedding package', and the only details I could remember from accounts on the Internet were no more or less tacky than those of any relationship seen from the outside. There were the slight anomalies, of course, like the fact that George had failed to turn up the first time the date had been set, having run off on a boozathon with another girl. But if the foundations for a long-lasting liaison based on mutual trust were absent, the hallmark of a certain authenticity was more evident than in most celebrity marriages. And although I found Alex's decision to marry George in the first place baffling, I could appreciate how she must have suffered. The life-and-soul-of-the-party drunk she had thought she married was now just a drunk, and it was as a pantomime clown that he was invited to attend functions – not as a celebrated former footballer. Their marriage, however, had lasted too long and overcome too many hurdles for it not to be based on genuine ties. After not yet two days with George, I knew that any woman who could stick by him for the best part of a decade would need a stronger incentive than *Hello!* magazine could provide.

'Because we were in a bad way,' George was saying slowly, staring at his glass as though blaming its emptiness for the slackening of his thought process, 'Alex started to believe all this crap in the papers. And I can't say I blame her.' He gestured for another drink. 'She'd always said that if there was one thing she wouldn't put up with it would be me cheating on her, but she knows how daft I get when I'm drinking – she knows that anything's possible. Still, you have no idea what it's like to watch the person you fell in love with turn into your mum, some woman who whinges on and on at you the second you get home until you think ...' He made a vague, capitulatory gesture. 'And then when the press joined in too, keeping on at me for the booze and the girls the way that they do, it just makes me want to stick two fingers up at the lot of them.' He watched, with bitter concentration, as a new spritzer began its journey from the bar top to the waiter's tray and towards him. 'Now that she's left me, I reckon I'm entitled to do just that, don't you? Whatever. I. Want.' The leer had crept back into his voice. 'If I want to grab life by the bollocks and have some fun, spend time with someone who isn't going to nag, why shouldn't I?' He took a sip – small and civilised, but of untold value – reached over and began to fondle my thigh.

Ignoring the building pressure of his hand, I ventured, 'You've had your fair share of fun though, George, haven't you?'

'Course I have, but I've been faithful to Alex for eight years, and since nobody seems to believe that, I might as well be the person everyone's so sure I am. That's what you do when you're a celebrity, isn't it?'

'What do you mean?'

'You give people what they want. Like that time on the Wogan show.'

The arrogance of these self-references had started to dilute themselves in my mind: was it still conceit if he was right? If

48

everyone really could remember the finer points of his life just as he imagined they did?

'The people at home, they wanted value for money, didn't they? So I just sat in that green room, with a full bar – I mean seriously, whose idea was that? – and I gave them what they wanted.'

'That's right.' It was coming back to me now, in the form of an anecdote my father had once told me. 'He asked you what you liked to do these days and you . . .'

'Told him the truth: screwing, I said.'

Through the material of my jeans shorts, I could feel him clumsily kneading away. Crossing my legs so his hand fell away, I asked, 'How do you know what you've done or haven't done, George? You've said yourself that you don't remember half the time.

'That's true,' he nodded, looking down at his spurned paw as though considering what to do with it now, titillated too, I suspect, by the challenge. 'And when you've been a bit of a boy your whole life, those instincts don't just vanish.' He put his glass down, surveyed the bar and whispered. 'I'll let you into a secret: I love women. I mean I *love* them.' His voice threatened to break with the emphasis, but he went on, 'People go on about me and blondes, but I like them all: tall, short, blonde or brunette. They've got to be beautiful, of course.'

'Of course,' I smiled, knowing that may have once been true but that now, those standards had been brutalised along with everything else.

'So, if Alex really has given up on me, I'm going to make the most of my opportunities.'

His bravado was pitiful.

'Do you keep in touch with your ex-wife?' I didn't need to know this, but as my self-consciousness around him lessened, curiosity was taking its place. Somewhere in between our first meeting and this moment, he had become real rather than a caricature, his personality a jumble of contradictory fragments that I wanted, despite myself, to piece together.

'What's it to you?'

He was distracted momentarily by a goal, then he turned a quizzical gaze back to me.

'Angie was an exceptional woman; she never did understand about the drink, though.'

He had been married to his first wife, a former Playboy bunny, for six years, before the booze and womanising finally prompted her to file for divorce. Just as I was about to point out that the only person likely to be understanding about the drinking was another drunk, he persevered.

'No matter how well she knew me – and she did know me – she always thought that it was just a question of me pulling myself together, when actually it was a little more complicated than that. And what was weird was that she did understand me – I mean, she knew from the start what made me tick, that I was an extreme person, and that I like to live every day like it's my last.'

I was dismayed by this last part, which had the tidy conceit of a sound bite; a botch of life rendered palatable for professional ears like mine. Or perhaps George had been famous for so long now that all his memories had been reduced to laminated offerings for public consumption.

'It was easier then,' he winked, garrulous all of a sudden, 'with other women. Journalists didn't just hop on planes like they do now, they didn't have these long lenses . . .'

'Those were the days eh, George?'

I had wanted to ask him about the boy, Calum, his twenty-two-year-old son with Angie, but the game had ended, the crowd's flat chanting giving way to a sudden flurry of conversation, and every eye was once again on George.

Detaching his back from the bar, where he'd been feeding himself peanuts with a mechanical gesture, one of the pool-playing journalists from the previous night sauntered towards our table.

'You all right, George?' Then, without waiting for an answer: 'We've got an exclusive from your missus going in tomorrow. I just wanted to say ..., well, mate, that I'm sorry.'

Satisfied that he had said his piece, he gave me a wink.

'Sorry about what, mate?' George raised a pair of bloodshot eyes from beneath the coarse tangles of their brows.

'Oh dear,' continued the journalist, cocking his head to one side. 'Hope I haven't put my foot in it. Alex has been telling everyone who'll listen that your marriage is over.' Dislodging a shard of peanut from a back tooth with his tongue, he added matter-of-factly: 'You messed up there, mate. She really is quite something.'

What came next happened so fast that I was, at first, only aware of a cold wetness in my lap as drinks skidded across the table. Looking up, I caught the full picture: George, a zigzag of blue vein carving up his forehead, was holding the journalist in a headlock 'I am not your mate, mate. And you want a comment from me about my marriage ending? I'll give you one: "So fucking what?"'

Observing the scene, the barman continued to dry his glasses, and from his small smile I gleaned that George could do no wrong, that this behaviour would only serve to cement his mythical status. The other journalists, meanwhile, and one couple in the far corner of the bar who affected astonishment but were secretly rejoicing in the distraction, had assumed placatory roles.

'Hey, hey, George – calm down!'

'George, come on – he's not worth it.'

Fingering the garland of white prints around his throat, the journalist retreated to the jukebox. 'Fucking nutball . . .'

George, still breathing heavily from the exertion, had snapped out of his daze and was looking at me with concern. Someone handed me a wad of kitchen towel.

'Sorry – you all right?' he asked. He sat back down into a pool of white wine and orange juice, and sprang back up again. 'Those little fuckers. Here – pass me some of that.'

There was a charged hush while the room begrudgingly registered that the entertainment was over, before low mutterings of conversation resumed. The level had grown loud again by the time George next spoke.

'I can't believe she really wants out.'

'Maybe you should talk to her yourself.'

We had been sitting there for hours and outside the sun – a smear of orange along the horizon – was bleeding out into the darkening sky. I'd lost count of the number of times I'd seen George motion, with the feeblest nod of the head, for another glass of wine, any attempt at conversation having dried up long ago. Still, observing him sitting there, eyes downcast, I felt something unnervingly like compassion.

'George?' It had lasted only an instant; all I could think of now was that I wanted this day to be over. 'Call her. Talk to her.'

Shrugging away my suggestion, he looked stonily back up at the TV screen. 'Out of interest,' each word was viciously enunciated, 'who the hell are you to say what I should and shouldn't do?'

He turned his eyes to me and I shivered: they were empty.

'And what do you know about my marriage? My life? You're all the same, you lot, you just want something nice and juicy to put in the paper.' He got up heavily, back rounded and eyes narrowed. 'Why don't you go back to your life and leave me to get on with mine.'

He made a move in the direction of the bar, then, thinking better of it, turned and disappeared down the narrow corridor leading to the gents.

Never having witnessed alcoholism in any form, I was stunned by this unprovoked spite. More baffling still was that I had felt his words deeply – as though they mattered. Just that morning, I had detected a desire to be looked after which had drawn me in; there had been an understanding, too, I had felt sure, that I was on his side. I didn't blame him for his outburst - journalists and the paparazzi would frequently wind up their subjects to get a reaction - but I did start to wonder where the drunk ended and George began. I only found out later that volatility had been a trait of his well before he discovered drink. His sister, Barbara, had told one interviewer that long before his genius on the pitch was recognised, their mother would spoil George far more than the other siblings, his looks elevating him above the rest even then.

'He's a slippery fish, isn't he?'

A benign-faced journalist in his forties sitting close by had overheard the whole thing.

'Isn't he just.' I began to gather my things.

'Wait – you're a journalist, aren't you?'

I looked uneasily towards the bathroom.

'Actually I'm just looking after him . . .'

'Right, right. But you're a journalist too, aren't you?'

I stood up and he followed.

'Listen, we're all in this together, right? Only I need to file something in the next few hours and what with this threat of divorce and so on, I wondered whether you could give me the inside track on . . .'

'I'm sorry.' The desk had warned me that this might happen, instructing me to share as little information as possible with 'the pack'. But standing there with this man who was in the same position as me, I felt like a schoolgirl portentously shielding her exercise book from a neighbour. 'I'm sorry,' I stammered. 'I really don't know any more than you do.'

Loitering outside the door leading to the toilets, I realised that I had been given the slip. Pushing through it and making my way along the narrow corridor, I knocked on the door of the gents.

'George?'

This was ridiculous; couldn't I let the man pee in peace?

'You looking for someone?'

Densely packed into his suit, the man had the physique of a rugby player and a docile, mismatched face. Following his invitation, I walked into his office. A laminated metal plaque, angled towards the empty leather chair into which I was motioned, put me at ease: 'General Manager, Shaun McCarthy'. The hotel manager, I had been told by the desk, was an old friend of George's who had worked in a

Manchester hotel popular with footballers in the seventies. He was firmly 'on side'.

'It's Celia, isn't it?'

Pushing the spine of his chair back as far as it would go, and taking his time before starting to speak, he appeared to be enjoying the situation. He nodded politely through my explanation, understanding my need to be there, before finally leaning forward, hands clasped solemnly together.

'At this point, George may need to be left alone for a bit,' he smiled. 'These guys,' he gestured in the direction of the bar, 'they're piranhas the bloody lot of them. You seem like a sweet girl, and God knows none of us want him to lose his contract with the paper.' Prising his hands apart, he inspected a hangnail. 'You know he's got no money, right? Lost it all about a decade ago – how he spent it I have no … actually, scratch that: I know full well how he spent it. Anyway, it started coming in again – the endorsements and the TV work – after the transplant, but all of that's going to go …' he whistled a trio of notes accompanied by the curling downward motion of a finger, 'now that he's drinking again, so he's largely dependent on your newspaper's paycheque. I don't know if you're aware, but it's not like he made a fraction of what these guys are on today.'

I must have nodded a little too fast, my desire to get out of that office and find George a little too obvious, because Shaun stopped talking.

'Do you know how much he used to earn at his peak at Manchester United?'

I thought about the hundred thousand pound a week footballers I read about and tried to formulate a guess in my head.

'A hundred pounds a week,' Shaun leaned back in his chair. 'Isn't that incredible? Best player the team's ever had, and that's what he got. The endorsements still meant he lived a nice life, but that's not really the point, is it?'

'No. He must feel pretty resentful.'

'Damn right he does. He feels he should have more to show for all those years. As it is, if Alex really does want a divorce, that could ruin him.'

'She won't go ahead with it, will she? After all this time?' I wasn't sure where these convictions of mine came from: I knew nothing about her or their situation. 'Is she really willing to sacrifice ...' I wanted to say 'being Mrs Best' but thought better of it, '... everything?'

'I don't know. When they got here everything was hunky-dory. The three of us went out for dinner to a local place and the pair of them were acting like loved-up teenagers. We were meant to go out again the following evening but Alex rang up, saying they'd had an argument, and that George had disappeared. Now, when he disappears,' he added with a grimace, 'there's only one thing he's doing, and Alex knows that. He's still taking his pills, is he?'

'I think so.'

'Good. I know he's drinking, but if he stops taking those into the bargain his body's just going to give up on him. I'm beginning to wonder if I shouldn't get Phil to come out here.'

'Phil is George's agent, right?' My boss had mentioned him.

'Well, best mate really. Picks him up off the floor when he's lost it, sorts him out with work even if he doesn't turn up half the time – the kind of guy we all need, George more than most. You should have him on speed dial.' He flicked through his Rolodex. 'Poor Phil. He and his wife have just had a baby boy; this is the one time in his life when he really doesn't need to be dropping everything for George. I was hoping I wouldn't have to bother him, but if things start to get out of hand we might have to haul him out here. He seems to be the one who can keep him in check.'

I was reassured by the 'we' and with Phil's number in my pocket ('Do me a favour, love and only use it in a real emergency – the poor guy's been up to his neck in this ever since the transplant'), I was ushered out of the office with the supple charm particular to the hospitality industry.

'Thanks for your help, Shaun.' I shook him by the hand. 'I'm sure you're right: I'll let him be this afternoon, then.'

Fifteen minutes later, I was walking briskly in the direction of The Lady Di, without the faintest prick of conscience. George could berate me as much as he wanted: I couldn't take the chance of leaving him alone.

George sat at the bar in exactly the same position as the night before, exuding menace. Any hint of complicity built up over the past twenty-four hours had vanished; I was afraid of him.

On the bar top lay a pile of that day's papers, to the right of which the barman, a younger man than on the previous night, had just placed a white wine spritzer with the concentration of a tightrope walker. George's presence was exercising so strong an effect on him that he was scarcely allowing himself to breath.

'I'll get that, George,' I said, remembering as I spoke that I wasn't allowed to buy him drinks.

He didn't betray a flicker of surprise.

'No, you won't,' he answered without looking up, pulling a thick wad of notes from his pocket and peeling two off. 'The day I let a woman pay for me, I really will be finished.'

Relieved, I climbed up on to the stool beside his, watching with concern as the sagging humps of his shoulders began to shake; was he choking? No: he was laughing. It started as a rumble in his throat and escalated into the great helium hiccups of an adolescent girl. It was unstoppable and infectious; two minutes later we were both wiping our eyes, a renewed sense of ease established.

'This is the best-kept secret in Sliema,' he nodded, pupils wet and pink-rimmed as a hound's. 'Nobody – until you came along, Trouble – could ever find me here.'

We sat in silence, and I registered the arrival of a Maltese couple who had frozen in recognition of George. I wondered at the nickname. Its objective, as with all nicknames, was to reassure, make me feel close, but there was also, I sensed, an apology implicit.

'I told them it was what you liked to drink,' said the barman, setting down a bottle of Chardonnay in an ice bucket before George with such feline insinuation that I almost expected him to offer his head to be stroked.

I watched as he gracefully acknowledged the gift, and it hardly seemed possible that this was the same man who had nearly throttled a stranger an hour ago. I wondered too about the jumbled ethics surrounding alcoholics. Would that same couple give a bottle to a drunk in the street? Of course not, but George wasn't just famous and drunk: he was a famous drunk. Like Paul Gascoigne, the very dependency he had acquired to deal with fame had become public property.

'Here.' Smirking, he pushed a Sunday tabloid he'd been flicking through along the bar. 'How do you reckon I look in this one?'

There was George, lying on a lounger, limbs oversaturated with colour, doing nothing. It could have been anybody or nobody for the information the image provided, but it was George. The text was correspondingly bland, the headline reading 'Best Relaxes After Wife Walks Out', but the implication was clear: the demise of George's eight-year marriage meant nothing to him.

'Oh yes,' he said after a long pause, looking up at me and setting off those dimples. 'I've still got it.'

CHAPTER THREE

With the assurance of alcohol, George had relaxed. Shards of anger from the earlier tantrum were still there, catching the light occasionally, but he had gone back to being someone I could sit beside without feeling afraid.

'I've always wondered whether the stars in those pictures secretly spend hours poring over them.'

'Hours, Celia. Anyone who tells you otherwise is lying. And if you're famous for being a good-looking man, you can't not think about it.'

My surprise at this boast must have showed; he was taking in my expression with amusement.

'What?'

'Nothing.'

'You not seen pictures of me when I was younger?'

'Course I have.' Although it hadn't, in fact, been until that morning, when one of the papers had run a picture of him in his early twenties.

'Well, I wasn't bad-looking, was I? What? Am I not allowed to say it? I remember one day in Miami, walking down the street and collecting thirty women's phone numbers.'

'George,' I was laughing, partly in admiration. Surrounded by cadgers and sycophants as he had been for the past thirty-five years, George would leave his natural modesty at the door when he'd had a drink. And he was right: it was difficult to guess from the way he looked now how beautiful he had once been. Examining the contours of his raffish face on the page, I had tried hard to imagine whether he might have appealed to me as a young man, but the dated style had made it impossible to tell.

'What do you want me to say?'

'Just that you appreciate being given a one-to-one with one of the world's prettiest men,' he laughed.

'Oh, I do,' I assured him.

'Funny.'

'What?' I said, skim reading an opinion piece about Alex's divorce threat in another paper.

'You couldn't really give a damn about me, could you?'

'You as a sixties pin-up?' I said evenly, relaxed enough to ask myself, for the first time, how long I would be asked to stay in Malta. 'No. And do you know what? I don't think I've ever seen you play.'

He was grinning so hard now that his eyes were slits.

'You don't think I . . . ? You think I'd know.'

'I'd hope so. Then again,' he shrugged, 'I don't really give a damn. It was a long time ago.'

'I do think you're funny,' I added, conscious that where his vanity was concerned that sense of humour might fail. 'Very funny, actually. I don't know why, but I wasn't expecting that.'

Without any warning, he leaned in towards me and placed a booze-scented kiss on the side of my mouth.

' "All Irishmen, particularly the actors, are very good at being Irish." Know who said that?'

'No.' If I was unfazed by the kiss, it was because I was enjoying his company. In the eighteen months I had worked as a journalist, I had always found the older subjects and interviewees – each of whom brought with them a little piece of history – the most rewarding. George's anecdotes were relevant to the present day too, and his perception of the world was never jaded, as it could so easily have become.

'Charlton Heston. Know why he said it? Because we are, as he put it, "both witty and funny". When asked what the difference was, he replied, "Wit is a matter of brains, funny is attitude." '

'And you, George, have plenty of both.'

Our eyes met and we held each other's gaze levelly, with a complete absence of subtext.

'George . . .'

'Hmm?'

'What are you going to do?'

He adopted a look of debonair insouciance.

'I thought I might just head off somewhere, the South of France maybe, or Spain, and spend the whole of August there. As my babysitter, of course, you'd have to follow me, so maybe we should hatch a plan together, eh?'

He gave me a nudge.

'Seriously, though. Won't you, at some point . . .' I was hesitant to bring it up and break our banter, '. . . need to go back to the hospital? Get checked up?'

'Not really.' He was lying and I knew it. 'I'm taking the pills, you know, just like they told me to, and anyway – what's waiting for me back in England, eh? A spitting mad wife, soon to be ex-wife, and a hefty legal bill. Why bother?'

Before I could probe more deeply into whether these were idle fantasies or concrete plans, the man standing at the other end of the bar and staring intently in our direction as he knocked back two brandies in swift succession, decided to make his approach.

'Excuse me, Mr Best?' The paper napkin he held in one outstretched hand was shaking. 'It's been my childhood dream to have George Best ask me for my autograph.'

'Can I have your autograph?' replied George, without missing a beat.

'Certainly.'

The man scribbled out his name, underlining it with a flourish, placed a ten euro note on the bar and left.

Spend any length of time intensively with a person and it's hard not to find some redeeming qualities there. That, at least, was what I told myself as we walked out of The Lady Di four hours later, having veered in and out of most subjects, from whether or not George's marriage could survive this new crisis to the one long-term relationship that gave me any credibility in such discussions.

'Do you still think about him?' he'd asked.

I'd been surprised at the question. 'Yes,' I replied, rather self-consciously.

'And you think of getting back with him?'

'No. Yes. Sometimes. We were too young to spend much longer together . . .'

'Too young? I love the way your generation speak. Angie was your age when I married her.'

'And look how that worked out.'

'Hey.'

There was no doubt about it, George Best was an easy man to like. What I hadn't bargained for was that his alcoholism would have its own endearing characteristics. Halfway though a drinking binge, I noticed that George would reach a kind of zenith of affability. There was nothing obviously drunk about his demeanour at that point; after four or five glasses, he was what the rest of us are after our first: pliable and optimistic. But the deeper he sank into it, the more irascible he became. Far from being anaesthetised like so many of us when we drink to excess, this tertiary stage of drunkenness would revive and stimulate him. Then came the delusions, the paranoia, the pointed 'theys' and the sombre looks. Pity the autograph hunter who braved his moment then, because although George would always do it, towards the end it would be with a black look that would send the fan scurrying away, clutching his bounty with a look of relief. What astonished me was that people always expected George to be as pleased to see them as they were to see him. 'What a coincidence,' they would exclaim, as though running into an old friend or relative in the most unlikely of places. 'Only it's not a coincidence though, is it?' George would whisper through clenched teeth to me once they'd left. 'Because I've no earthly idea who you are.'

It would have been too easy for the day to end there. Back at the hotel, standing beside him, willing the lift to arrive, I could feel it coming.

'One more for the road?'

In the bar, the other journalists, bored of looking for

George, their papers put to bed, had embarked on binges of their own.

'George …' I knew that the pleading in my voice would only serve to remind him exactly why he didn't need someone like me around. 'It's late, why don't we …'

But I was talking to myself. He was already walking away from me, jangling the change in his pocket, like any other holidaymaker opting for an innocent nightcap.

'It's George Best,' a tourist, imbecilic with amazement, stood facing him at the bar. 'I can't believe it. Gabby, come and look who it is: George Best.' Content, apparently, to stare at this chimerical character from close quarters, repeating his name rather than attempting to talk to him, he and his wife settled nearby, gazing like birdwatchers at a rare specimen for the remainder of the night.

'People are weird,' I muttered to him under my breath. 'How can you stand it?'

'Oh, I don't even notice any more,' he said distractedly. 'What I do mind is that, there.' I followed his gaze to a young woman bending to retrieve cigarettes from a machine, revealing, as she did so, a pagan symbol tattooed on the small of her back. I threw him a quizzical look. 'Tattoos,' he shrugged. 'I can't stand them. Why would you ruin your body like that?'

I turned to look at her. She was young, about nineteen, in low-slung bootleg jeans and Converse, and it occurred to me that most young men would see her as a beacon of desirability.

'Alex,' he shook his head, the mere mention of her name bringing back everything he was trying to forget, 'she was always worrying about her breasts being too small, when they were perfect, perfect. Kept threatening to have them done, and I told her: do that and I'll leave you. I like my women natural.' Running his eyes caressingly over my frame, he added in a silky voice, 'Like you.'

It was a quarter to two in the morning, and the warm air carried in a faint sea smell of sulphur through the open windows. George's roguish patter had started up again, and a vague resentment had begun to permeate the tiredness. The advantages of being a girl in this scenario were all too obvious. Yet I felt a little jealous of the male reporters, who could enjoy a very different bond with him.

I was saved from having to deliver yet another wry repartee by a German businessman who invited George to play a game of pool. The best of three turned into the best of five and by the time they had finished playing, I could barely keep myself awake. George, however, was still surrounded on all sides by journalists waiting for him to show signs of either tiredness or excessive drunkenness – any state which would make him more vulnerable to a quick blast of interrogation. But drinking seemed to imbue George with superhuman traits, make him stronger and more alert rather than limp and bleary like the rest of us.

'Anyone for another game?' George was addressing the room, the overture sounding more like a threat than a question, and I wondered whether he too could sense that the room was turgid with tension.

A Scottish tourist, his freckled face a riot of russet, obscured my vision. 'Bloody sad state of affairs this whole business with George,' he shook his head, gazing expectantly up at me all the while for any detail which might help him quantify just how sad a state of affairs it was. 'I mean, me and the wife had been reading about it in the papers and then there he is, in the same hotel as us.'

I nodded distractedly; the sound of an abusive Irish voice had perforated the even throb of conversation. Standing with his arms crossed before the journalist who had provoked him earlier, shoulders low and feline, George was growling, 'Why are you still here?'

'Now, I'm his number one fan,' the freckled tourist went on, oblivious, 'but I've got to say that I do feel for that lovely wife of his.'

'Excuse me,' I murmured, rounding the bar just in time to see George grab an empty beer bottle by the neck and smash it down hard on the edge of the pool table. Before he could use it, the journalist, younger and more agile than him, placed his hands neatly, side by side, on George's chest and propelled him backwards.

'Cool it, mate – all right?'

Not to be outdone, George charged forwards, stumbled and crumpled in on himself, falling hard against the bar top. With a sound of slewed gristle, his nose caught the mahogany ledge as he went down.

Strange how in control one can feel when things go wrong. I walked over to George, helped him up, and sat him down on a bar stool, asking the barman for something to stem the blood and mucus running down over his lips and chin and on to his T-shirt. When I did speak, my voice sounded calm, and George didn't protest when, with a tea towel held up to his nose, I guided him away.

Listening to him cracking jokes as I cleaned him up in his room, I wondered whether in some perverse way he had enjoyed what had just happened. Psychiatrists talk of the relief addicts can feel at having their pain externalised – localised to something as precise as a nosebleed. I had settled him on the bed, plugged his nostrils with cotton wool, and was busy texting the office when George got up precipitately, ran to the toilet and began to throw up.

Only then – pacing the room and trying to block out the dry chokes and thick, mucus splutters – did I feel a flutter of alarm. How much of this was out of the ordinary? Should I call reception and ask them to fetch a doctor? Or would that simply turn this into a bigger incident than it already was? I tried to imagine myself as the unflappable reporter I hoped to be years from now, but it seemed unimaginable that anyone could remain cool under these circumstances. As the retching grew louder, I pulled a folded Post-it from my pocket. Covering one ear with a hand, I dialled the number scrawled across it.

'Phil?'

That was a long night. Unable to leave George in the state he was in, I settled in an armchair at the foot of the bed, pulling my knees tightly to my chest, listening out until I heard his laboured breath fall into an even rhythm. At some point during the non-time which is neither night nor morning, George had risen from the bed in a semi-slumber, stumbled over to the minibar and tried, cursing all the while, to break it open before giving up and going back to bed. Even in his dreams, it was all about the drink.

It was late when I woke up, nearly eleven, and I couldn't move my neck. Looking over at him lying prone on the bed, his clothes twisted like ligatures around his torso, the expression on his face unapologetic even in sleep, I felt angry. I wanted to go home.

Taking in the bloodied towel lying on the floor by a bedside table littered with empty sweet packets, I wondered at my decision to spend the night in George's room. For a night to end as it had must not be unusual for George and perhaps I should have seen it coming. But what could I have done? I imagined a conversation with my editor in which I told him that a man would be better suited to this job, but the prospect alone made me feel like a failure. And I would have failed. No, I would swallow the panic and focus on the flashes of charisma, the pale reminders of the legend I had read about: they were what made this job worth completing. Looking over at his shape beneath the bedclothes, I couldn't shake off the idea that the essence of him was already gone. An image of the hollowed-out crab shells I would find on the beach as a child, fraudulently intact, with sometimes even the eyes still there, came to me. The sound of someone wrestling with a key-card in the lock, followed by a gentle cursing, roused me from my thoughts.

With a final push, the door broke open and a pale man in his forties dangling a 1980s sports bag, the glossy leather chipped with age, walked into the room. His lips were clamped shut in the manner of someone with a job to do, but there was humour in his features: irony in that bloodless mouth and generosity of spirit in his tortoiseshell eyes.

'Celia, is it?' Setting down the bag he held out a hand. 'Phil.'

I shook it gratefully. 'You have no idea how relieved I was to hear that you were already on your way. I'm so sorry you were bothered, though: Shaun mentioned that you'd just had a baby. Congratulations.'

'Thank you.' Kneading the back of his neck with one hand, he looked over at George, still breathing heavily into the crook of his arm.

'Your office had warned me that things were getting worse. I should probably have come out earlier. How's Beastie?'

'Well, his nose has stopped bleeding, so that's something.'

Shuddering out a laugh, he sank on to a nearby chair. A minute passed, a minute Phil used to look me up and down and take in the blood-soaked tea towel, his expression unreadable.

'You must have been having a whale of a time,' he said finally.

I sat down opposite him, relieved. The reinforcement I needed was here.

'I'm sorry I had to call you, Phil. I know that you ... well, Shaun had said not to bother you unless it was an emergency but since the office ...'

'Oh, I'd say this qualifies.' Phil gave another grimace. 'Problem is, it always does. Now, do you know what I think you need?' He reached for the leather-bound room service menu lying on the coffee table. 'A good fry-up – just look at you,' he winked, extending his mouth into a smile-like shape, even if the impulse behind it wasn't there. 'So, do we reckon these are smoking rooms?'

They weren't and, having ascertained with a muttered expletive that the windows were sealed shut, Phil picked up the phone and ordered two fried breakfasts (George rarely ate them) and some cereal for his friend.

When he was done, he edged off his shoes, dropped back down into the armchair and, with a rhetorical 'Do you mind?', lit a cigarette. The nicotine mollifying his voice, he recounted quickly, out of necessity rather than a desire to confide, I felt, how he and George had met. Phil had been doing a crossword at the bar of a Mayfair bar, Blondes, popular in the 1980s, when George had walked in. 'It sounds silly, but before I even turned around, I could feel his presence. Then he came up, sat down next to me and said, "struggling with that, are we?" ' With lassitude and suppressed emotion he described George's ascent from the slight, timid young prodigy he once was to the global star he became (still timid, but drinking heavily to drown the fact). George, he maintained, could always find a reason to celebrate or commiserate. Finally, his speech punctuated with facts, he described the realisation (first Phil's, then George's) that his friend had turned into an alienating alcoholic. He and the family had sought help of every imaginable kind ('Only he needed to help himself, before anyone else could'), then finally there was the transplant and the new lease of life that it represented.

'George saw his new liver as the blessing that it was; he didn't take that second chance lightly. But what a lot of people don't get is that his is not just an addiction to booze,' Phil added pragmatically. 'Pubs and everything that comes with them are a part of George's soul.'

'I think George used those exact same words,' I smiled.

'It's true. It wasn't that he spent time in them as a lad, but during his twenties he really fell in love with them. One of the things he found hardest after the transplant was being able to sit there chatting to people without a drink in his hand. But that didn't mean he couldn't get through it – he just needed to stick it out.'

There was an energy and an optimism about Phil that belied his slouched frame and beaten expression, and I warmed to him immediately. I liked the way he talked in

clichés, each one trotted out with the conviction of someone who had assembled that particular pattern of words for
the first time, and I admired his loyalty to George, even if,
from what I'd seen, he didn't deserve it. Phil's allegiance to
George, I could see as I watched him call his wife to check
on her and the baby, went beyond blood ties. Not for the
first time, he had dropped everything to come and rescue
his friend.

CHAPTER FOUR

'WHEN GEORGE AND ALEX first moved out to Surrey,' Phil explained through a mouthful of egg, 'I really thought he might have cracked it. That was one of the longest stretches he had ever managed without drinking. He'd found this local pub he liked ...'

'The Chequers?'

'That's right. And people used to come from miles around to see him, knowing that they might get a chance to talk to George Best, or just have a good ogle - and he liked that. It made him feel like everything didn't have to change just because he had a Diet Coke in his hand.' Phil yapped out a smoker's cough that turned into a laugh. 'All these footballers nowadays in their fancy bars ... George would never have fitted in.'

A noise from the tangle of limbs on the bed – a moist rearrangement of lips and tongue – prompted us to look over at the sleeping figure, and Phil fell silent for a moment.

'You see, that's what I don't get about George.'

Phil reached for another cigarette. 'What's that?'

'These young players in the papers always pictured coming

out of Bond Street shops with their bags or falling out of nightclubs: it feels like they're relishing the attention. I can never decide if George does or not.'

'He didn't, at first, because he was such a shy lad. Then he learned to like it and now I don't think he knows either way. He's naturally a very private man, but it depends too on how much he's had to drink.'

My phone made a drilling noise from the table: a text from the office ('Update?').

'Had he not been ...' I hesitated to say 'flawed' in front of Phil. 'Had he not had this disease – what do you think he might have done?'

'I think he could have done a great deal more back home – he's one of the most revered figures in Northern Ireland, you know – and I think he still could, if he could just come through.'

'Can't you and Alex work together to make him stop? Both of you threaten to leave him or something?' I wouldn't have resented a scathing response, aware of how simplistic this sounded, but Phil's answer was straight.

'Alex is a great girl – she really has been through the mill – and we've tried everything together and separately, but it's like the experts say: unless you want to give up, nothing and no one is going to make you.'

'So the stints in rehab ...?'

'They'd work for a while: he'd come out, having lasted a day longer than the previous time, just to prove that he could, just to mess with you, and then he'd start drinking again. We knew we were just playing for time.' Letting his eyes close, he shook his head slowly. 'Ah, the plans we had; the deals we were going to sign off this year.'

A maid had come to take the breakfast plates away, leaving George's - untouched beneath its silver dome - on the side. As the trays were fussed over, I wondered why he couldn't simply retire. I knew from Shaun that George had had his difficult patches, but after nearly forty years of fame, how hard up could he be?

I decided to come straight out and ask. 'What's his financial situation, Phil? I mean, I know he told me that what he made as a footballer was a pittance compared to these guys now, but surely all the Sky punditry and the adverts, the after-dinner speeches and the endorsements . . . ?' My father had told me about the billboards: clothing, aftershave and chewing gum, world-famous brands that buckled beneath the weight of his image; George remembered long after they were forgotten.

'Well, there's the drinking and the gambling, then there's the constant apologising to Alex (that doesn't come cheap), and the healthcare, which isn't going to get any less expensive in years to come. He's had run-ins with the bailiffs several times in the past so now I've just got to keep him on the straight and narrow. The column he does for you guys is the best-paid job he's got – and the safest. That's why I'm happy for you to be here and willing to help you out.'

That week, Phil added grimly, the calls had started coming in from the magazines, radio stations and TV shows for whom George regularly worked. 'They're never from the top dog, who promised George the moon when they first signed him up. No, these are from someone else, someone I've never spoken to before, telling us that George "isn't right" for them any more.' He looked past me at the clean wash of sky visible between the brocade hotel curtains and the deeper stripe of Mediterranean blue beneath. 'You're wondering why on earth I do it, aren't you?'

'Yes.' I smiled gently, anxious not to offend him.

'He's my best friend, has been for half a lifetime. The problem with George is that he doesn't really give a stuff about money – never has done – until he doesn't have any left. "I came here with nothing and I'll go home with nothing," he says when I have a go at him. But I'll tell you something: if you're lucky enough to get to know him even a little, you'll see why I'll always stick by him.' He stood up and patted his trouser pockets for his cigarettes. 'Now then, let's get the Beast up, out of here and back home, shall we?'

'He won't go, Phil,' I shook my head. 'He seems determined to—'

Mid-drag, Phil silenced me with a hand. 'He will go. George may not always let me tell him what to do, but he will listen. He'll see that the sensible option is to get him into hospital or rehab, somewhere there are professionals to keep an eye on him. And if he won't agree to that, I'll have to get his physician to come and see him in Surrey.'

'And he'll do that?'

'Most people will do most things where George Best's concerned. So here's what we're going to do: you're going to go downstairs and check the two of you out.' He shot me a meaningful look. 'I'm assuming the paper has generously offered to foot George's bill here?'

I nodded; Phil was good.

'Meanwhile I'll get him together—'

'And we'll meet in reception in what, half an hour or so?'

He threw me a crooked smile. 'You haven't been doing this long, have you? No, we want to get George out of here without a scene. I'm not looking to have the whole circus in tow all the way back to Surrey.'

'Oh.' I felt like an idiot. 'Of course . . .'

'There's a fire escape at the end of this corridor; I checked it out on my way here. The stairs go right down to the kitchen. So we'll meet just inside the door in . . .' he looked over at George with a mixture of fondness and annoyance, '. . . say forty minutes? That'll give me time to get a car sorted too.'

'I can do that,' I volunteered, anxious to redeem myself, 'while I'm checking out I'll . . .'

But Phil was shaking his head. 'Backhanders, Celia. In my experience they all tip the press off, everywhere you go, every hotel in the world. Leave the car to me, and with any luck, we'll make it out of here without the drama. But if you could let Shaun know what we're up to – discreetly, please – while you're down there, that might be a help.'

Once in the lift, I called the office.

'You did the right thing calling in Phil,' my boss sounded relieved. 'And George'll be much safer back here.' I waited, anxiously, for him to say it. 'Well, it looks like your little adventure might be coming to an end. Call me when you land.'

I didn't dare reply in case he changed his mind.

George was monosyllabic; a little boy whose bravado vanishes the second his mother appears. Dressed haphazardly in shorts, a dress shirt (the only clean thing he had left), black socks and trainers, I sensed contrition beneath his gruffness.

'Did you manage to get him to take his pills?' I whispered to Phil as George and Shaun jangled on ahead down the fire escape.

'Oh yes. You know, he's actually pretty good about them.'

I smiled. 'I'm in awe. How can you be so laid-back?'

'Practice. And you know, he reacts much better if you're relaxed.'

I could see that. With everyone but Phil it felt like George was testing the boundaries; with his friend, he knew quite clearly where they were.

At the bottom of the staircase, Shaun was holding the door open and ushering us into what looked like a pantry. George, I realised from a surreptitious glance at his face, had begun to enjoy himself.

'This is like *Goodfellas*, eh?' he whispered as our shambolic procession moved through a stainless steel world complete with kitchen staff looking up in wonderment from their pans to see one of the world's most famous footballers scurrying past a few feet away. 'Except there would have to be a shoot-out, right?'

He elbowed me in the ribs, trying to gauge whether I was annoyed with him about the previous night.

'Hey.' I could hear his breath, shallow and excitable, behind me. 'You angry with me?'

Had I not been so tired, I might have turned around and mustered a smile, but last night's scene – that stupid, pointless fight – had been avoidable, and could have ended far more seriously. It riled me too that George seemed to have been let off so easily and that Phil had been able to subdue him in an instant. But the consciousness that I was caught up in it all – that I cared – annoyed me more. I kept my expression immovable as the three of us were led by Shaun into a small alleyway behind the hotel.

'Ah – here's the car.'

While Shaun dispensed instructions to the driver, George turned to Phil. 'Mate? What is it that you always say is the most irritating thing about women?'

'That they tell you nothing's wrong when something clearly is,' Phil flung back automatically, hoisting George's bags up into the trunk of the car.

'Correct.'

George was looking at me triumphantly now, and gesturing flamboyantly into the back seat.

'Except that I never said a word,' I protested.

But he was grinning triumphantly. 'Ladies first.'

'I'm telling you, a gentleman would never say how many women he's slept with.'

Heckling from Phil, who was fingering his cigarette packet longingly with one hand, greeted this comment.

We had been driving for twenty minutes and the driver, a hexagonal-faced local with a Dali moustache, hadn't stopped talking. He was, he assured us in broken English, George's number one fan. After listing a series of his successes, goals, and legendary drunken moments ('When you stepped off the plane in Manchester wearing your sombrero, man ...') he had, with a gall that had in turn been entertaining, baffling, then faintly irksome, begun to question El Beatle on the subject of women.

'I always thought that model, Angie Lynn – you were engaged to her, weren't you? – was a beautiful girl. But then what about that Miss World? Mary something? Posed naked on a horse for that famous photographer? Back then, I was working as a mechanic and we had that picture pinned up in the staff kitchen. Every time one of us walked by it we would say, "George is one lucky man." Hey, can I ask you something?'

'Something tells me you're going to,' grunted George, as he worked his way through the box of Maltesers casually proffered at the start of the journey.

'How many were there in all? I mean,' he persevered, as though it were in need of clarification, 'how many have you had in your time?'

I laughed and looked over at George, who bared teeth covered in a viscous reddish film, and began pushing back finger after finger, counting aloud.

'Seriously, George.' I couldn't help it; I was curious. 'What are we talking: a thousand? More than that? Couldn't have been more than that ...'

'Listen, you two.' George was laughing now. 'Three things. One, I would never say, not in front of a lady,' he gave me a wink. 'Two, "my time"? This is still my time, thank you very much, so I couldn't give you a finite number. And three, just for the record, you're not even close.'

The driver squawked delightedly, storing up George's answer like a windfall he would later share with his friends, and we drew up outside Malta airport.

The journey through check-in and security took six minutes – I timed it. So this was what fame meant: an already good life made easier. Having taken George's ticket and realised, with a look not dissimilar to fear in his eyes, that this was indeed George Best, the BA clerk started up muted mutterings into a headset. Within seconds, a Maltese lady with a badge proclaiming herself the 'Special Guest Relations Director' appeared and ushered us through back corridors and doors marked 'private' into the first-class lounge. There, businessmen and wealthy holidaymakers tried desperately to recompose their faces and address the tasks at hand: reading their papers with studied concentration, ambling over to the food and beverage counter, eyes firmly averted from a man whose celebrity was so great that it risked demeaning them.

Taking in the well-stocked bar in the centre of the room with the fatalistic expression of a mother whose toddler has manoeuvred itself within reaching distance of a box of indelible markers, Phil sank down on a sofa and waited. One of George's punch lines, with all the singsong cadence of those Irish vowels, drifted across to us from the corner of the room, where an audience had already assembled: 'So I told the man, "That don't-you-know-who-I-am moment? That's when you're in serious trouble." '

'You OK, Phil?' I asked. The skin around his eyes had the greenish, iridescent quality of a bruise, and I remembered that he had made the journey to Malta at personal cost.

He looked questioningly at me.

'I mean, your wife can't be thrilled ...'

Phil shrugged. 'It wasn't easy leaving my little boy behind, so for him to kick off now really wasn't ideal. But well ...' He gave a tight smile and reached for another newspaper. The expression on his face suddenly lifted. 'You seen this?' He held up the tabloid he was reading.

It was a full-page picture of me and George by the pool, with the headline 'George and Mystery Blonde as Wife Files for Divorce'.

I tried to smile but my mouth felt stiff. 'What does the piece say?'

Phil emitted a gurgle of amusement as he read aloud. ' "The two were inseparable," said one eyewitness. "After the girl had finished giving him a tender massage, they disappeared inside the hotel." '

'Tender massage? I was rubbing sun cream into ... and we went in to watch ...' I gave up, knowing anything I said would sound disingenuous. 'I guess it serves me right,' I attempted, with a pragmatism I didn't feel, trying not to picture the laughter back home at the paper's morning conference. Only then did I think of Alex who, I hoped, would know that I was a journalist – not some girl her husband had picked up minutes after her departure.

'Don't worry about her,' said Phil, reading my mind. 'I'll make sure she knows who you are.'

'Thanks.'

'Look at you,' he was scrutinising me, 'you're all put out, aren't you?'

'I'm not.'

'I hate to rubbish your industry,' his eyes were smiling but his mouth was serious, 'but it's all fish and chips paper tomorrow, and maybe it's not such a bad thing for you to be on the receiving end for once. Everyone knew you were a journo, they were just having a laugh at your expense.'

He picked up the paper, examined the picture once more and suppressed another snort.

'You've got to admit: it is quite funny. But anyone who knows George would know that there was nothing in it.'

'Exactly.'

'You're far too old for him.'

We were still laughing when George drifted over.

'You two fancy anything?'

An urgency I was starting to recognise had infiltrated George's face and limbs, as though a current of electricity,

82

constant but of fluctuating intensity, were coursing though him. With his pigeon-toed walk, those trainers squeaking a little against the parquet floor, he headed meekly in the direction of the bar.

'Mate?'

George stopped and turned to face his friend.

'We're not going to get into a situation where they won't let you on the flight, are we?'

A look passed between the two men in which resentment, defiance, admiration and the suppressed desire to laugh were all present.

'No, Hughsie, we're not.'

'It could be a long journey,' said Phil, returning to his newspaper.

As it turned out, George couldn't have been more docile or amenable than during that three-hour flight. Maybe it was the pills doing their work, but after his ritualistic banter with the air hostesses — proof to George that he was still the debonair good-timer of yesteryear — he dropped off, his mouth falling open in a pensioner's gape. Lucky for him that he failed to notice the fond pity which had replaced the swoons, or realise that the extra pillow handed to him by the youngest and prettiest member of staff was done with the smile she probably reserved for her grandfather. Oblivious to it all, he slept on, his head lolling on to my shoulder, where I let it rest.

'Goodbye, George.'

Sitting on a trolley by the baggage carousel, his good humour slept off, George picked disconsolately at a scab on his ankle, an excuse not to look up.

'Bye.'

I felt none of the elation I had anticipated, just an acute tiredness – and a niggling concern for George.

'Is he going to be all right?' I whispered to Phil, kissing him goodbye on the cheek.

'I'll see that he is. We'll get the doctor over, see what's what and, if we can, get him into rehab.' He looked doubtful.

A trio of bags fell with lumpen thuds on to the carousel, George's among them.

'Come on then, mate.'

I watched the two of them follow the signs through Nothing to Declare. They were of roughly the same height, though Phil was stockier than George and seemed to exercise a sensory command over his friend, leading him on through eye contact alone. A spatter of flashbulbs greeted them, masts and microphones descending on George with curiously elegant symmetry. I had wanted to say one last goodbye here, force some kind of reaction from George, but through the elbows, backpacks, waxy jackets and metal machinery I could see that a scuffle had broken out. Seconds later the two men had reached a car with blacked-out windows waiting outside the terminal, and I saw Phil gently pushing down on George's head as he climbed into the backseat, the way policemen do with their charges on TV.

'I've only been back a day.' It sounded more plaintive than I had wanted. Besides, that day – the first back at the office – had been a long one. From the moment I'd let myself into my empty flat the night before, a feeling of anticlimax had lingered.

'I know you have, but you've built up a rapport with him and I've cleared it with Phil: they're expecting you.'

I thought of George and the memory of his expressionless face at the airport filled me with malaise.

'I'm not sure we did build that much of a rapport.'

But that wasn't what they wanted to hear. The bigger the story grew, the more important it became to keep the columnist who was at the centre of it all. He was, after all, the most newsworthy drunk in Britain. Within the hour, I was on the A3 heading to Surrey, without even a toothbrush or a change of clothes.

'Get whatever you need down there and charge it,' I'd been told. 'There isn't time for you to go home. George has been telling anyone who'll listen that he's delighted his marriage is over, that he was bored of Alex and is ready to move on. The place has been surrounded all day: George can't take a slash right now without everyone knowing about it and we need you on the inside.'

Just over an hour later I pulled into a narrow lane leading down to a small close of five or six single-storey, flintstone houses. The place must have been a large farm once. Now it was a cluster of lavishly converted barns, occupied in the majority, I imagined, by wealthy city boys who made the commute to London every day as their wives lounged in the shallows of the local health club pool. It was late afternoon and the sky, threatening rain, lit up the neat chimneys and bay windows with the artificial, electric light of a stormy summer's day. George's house was easy to spot, surrounded as it was by a picket line of paparazzi, rising now, with varying degrees of inquisitiveness, from their hunched positions on the front lawn.

'Well, hello again.' Phil was holding the door open and motioning me in. 'Bet you didn't think you'd be back so soon.'

His smile was gracious but weary, and I wondered whether

he'd been home yet. I followed his gaze to George, who was busy checking that the blinds were pulled down as far as they would go, and my immediate impression was that this was a different man to the untamed soul I had met in Malta.

'Hey,' George threw me casually, and I realised with an involuntary prick of disappointment that I had been right: he and I had no rapport. We were, to one another, just a means to an end. When they disappeared into the kitchen (I could imagine Phil's 'Be nice, George, be nice'), I took advantage of the moment to cast my eye over the recently renovated duplex, its sculpted wooden balcony overlooking a carefully thought-out sitting room. Most of the room – the hearth, with its antique brass andirons; the Burmese teak table and large antique rocking horse – jarred so completely with my perception of George as a misfit, an insubordinate who could not be pushed down into the rigid confines of existence, that I moved around it in a daze. The book-shelves, however, were pure George. Paperback thrillers, swollen, dog-eared and grease-spotted with use, were spine to spine with leather-bound classics by Lawrence, Wilde and Hemingway, while the whole of one lower shelf was filled with general knowledge books: *What You Know, You Know, Exercise Your Mind* and *The Dictionary of Trivia*. Beside a wedge of dictionaries and thesauruses, one book, *Learn Spanish in a Month,* had been pulled from the shelf in a fit of self-improvement and then abandoned. Two large sofas, scattered with cushions and throws, and a mahogany coffee table replete with a fan of magazines, took up the greater part of the room, but the centrepiece was George's trophies.

Showcased on a large Welsh dresser, the dozen or so cups and awards of varying shapes and sizes had been kept conspicuously polished – Alex's pride in them possibly approximating George's – and yet rather than exude achievement, they seemed to weigh as heavily on the atmosphere as the ashes of a deceased relative.

'Fancy a cup of tea?' Fresh from his pep talk, George was smiling; a middle-aged homebody in jeans and a striped shirt.

'Why not?'

'I'm going to leave you two to it,' Phil announced.

'Really? Why don't you stay?' The mere mention of him leaving had prompted a mild panic in George, and I wondered at the purity of his selfishness. 'I might need you to defend my honour again.'

The two men burst out laughing.

'Did you see Phil punching that photographer at the airport?' George asked me, by way of explanation.

'I thought I saw something kicking off . . .'

'Yeah. That was Phil. It was me who had to calm him down for a change.'

'Trust me: the irony wasn't lost on me,' Phil smiled. 'But I can't stay, mate.' He was already shrugging on a black leather jacket. 'I've got to get back home. Besides, you've got your sitter now,' he cocked his head in my direction. 'I never asked how much you charge. Ten quid's the going rate these days, no?'

'Something like that,' I rejoined. 'But it goes up if the charge stays up past his bedtime.'

We all laughed, but beneath the jokes our simmering discomforts were obvious. Phil should have been with his new baby, not here with George, but his friend's marriage looked done for, along with his career prospects if he didn't give up the booze. And then there was me, trying to work out which of my wildly contradictory emotions should take precedence. Six months ago I would have given anything to find myself in the middle of a situation that was captivating the newspaper-reading public. If only I could focus on the excitement I had felt as I neared the barn, and not on the fear of being left here with this unpredictable man. But to do that I needed to be clear in my mind how I felt about George, and not waver, as I did when I looked at him now, between fear, compassion and indifference.

'Any problems,' said Phil, giving me a quick hug on the doorstep, 'just call. Right?'

'Why are you smiling?'

'Am I?' Perched on the arm of the sofa, I watched George move about the room. 'It's just all so surprising, George. You, this place, the tea making.'

'Is it?' He disappeared into the kitchen. 'I don't see why. Where did you think I lived? In a nightclub? Did you imagine that I spent my life in hotel bars getting pissed?'

'Yes.'

He chuckled. 'Well, I don't. If I hadn't been a footballer I would have been quite happy being somebody's househusband.'

'Oh, please.'

'What? I would.'

Flicking though a biography of George's which had been published the previous year, and wondering what it must be like to read your own life story told in the words of another, it took me a second or two to register the gag. Standing behind me, back-lit by the neon kitchen lights, George was holding a cup of tea in each hand, wearing a small yellow pinny.

'This is the George people need to see,' I croaked, once we had both stopped laughing. *And this is the George I can deal with,* I thought to myself.

Later, as he made us cheese on toast while barking out answers to *Who Wants to be a Millionaire* from the kitchen, I examined the series of photographs dotted about the room. The largest, a black and white portrait of the happy couple on their wedding day, showed a full-faced and bearded George grinning demonically as he vaunted his gorgeous bride for the camera. The hounded look was there in his eyes and I wondered, casually, if he had been drunk when it was taken. Alex was unrecognisable from the recent pictures I'd seen of her in the papers. Eyes not yet dulled and lips heavy-rimmed as a teenager's, she squinted shyly at the camera. The snap had all the unhappy prescience of pictures of the dead on the news, where the person's tragic fate seems obscenely obvious to you, an idle onlooker. Other photographs, later in the marriage, were not so loaded, although Alex's expression seemed to become steadily more knowing as time went by. In the most recent pictures, she had adopted the savvy, elongated body shape of a model, those eyes – rendered impenetrable with kohl – staring hungrily at the camera. The latest photograph of the couple had – judging by the formality of their smiles – been taken by an outsider, someone who had never seen Alex run from the room in tears, or the ex-footballer give his wife's shoulders a not-so-gentle shake. In the picture George was standing while Alex, looking alarmingly thin in low-slung jeans and a T-shirt, was crouching down, massaging one of the dogs' jowls. Something in the tense angling of her body, however, seemed to suggest a recent wrong George had committed.

My phone rang, my boss's brusque tones interrupting my conjectures.

'You there yet? How is he?'

George reappeared, shooting a quick glance at the huddled shapes behind his blinds, trilling like crickets in the darkness.

'Fine – I mean, under control.'

Whistling quietly, George extended himself on the sofa.

'Excellent. Phil was right to get him back home. Now listen, I know this whole thing is dragging on, but you'll just have to brave it another day or two. Is he drinking?'

I looked over at George, sucking on a pencil with *The Times* crossword on his lap.

'No,' I stuttered, irritated by the metamorphosis.

'Broadcaster heard in an island – any ideas?' George called out.

I covered the mouthpiece. 'Sorry, George – be with you in two secs.'

A laugh crackled through the earpiece. 'Was that him? What does he want?'

'Nothing – just a crossword clue.'

'Christ. Doing the crossword with George Best. What so many men would give to be in your position.'

I flushed and moved through into the kitchen.

'He hasn't always been this easy. This is pretty much the first time since I went out to Malta that he's not been on the rampage.'

'So here's the plan.' My boss wasn't listening. 'Your job is to make sure he doesn't speak to anyone except his ghost-writer. And if that doesn't happen, we'll just stick a footnote in saying "George Best is away". Better still: "George Best is off his head in a bar somewhere and we have no idea when he'll be back" – just in a very small font.'

I didn't laugh. 'Fine.'

'Seriously, though, we need him to calm down, lay off the booze and get back to his column as soon as possible. He was doing so well, wasn't he? I really thought . . .' He paused. 'You're OK down there, right?'

He had asked the question out of politeness rather than concern, but instead of feeling affronted, I admired his coolness. When I started out as a journalist I would never have imagined that any job could be as intimate or emotionally complex as this one. Yet there would come a time, I assumed, when, like my colleagues, little would faze me. I looked forward to it.

'Yes,' I smiled. 'I'm fine.'

'I'll check in tomorrow then,' he sounded relieved. 'Goodnight.'

'Any ideas, then?'

I joined George on the sofa.

'I'm sorry?'

'Broadcaster heard in an island – it's my last one.'

I looked over – one eight-box space was left blank, the others filled with George's wild lettering.

'You did all that just now?' I was distracted and he could tell.

'Everything OK at the office?'

'Yes.' I looked down at the two toasted cheese sandwiches on the table and back up at George. 'But they want a column out of you – whenever you feel up to it, of course.'

'Sure,' he was fiddling with the remote, flicking silently through the channels, apparently unperturbed. 'I can put some stuff together tomorrow with David.'

A photograph I hadn't noticed earlier of a teenage George playing football sat on a side table by the television. His leg was extended in a kicking motion, the muscles defined with equine clarity, and his thick dark hair fell in stripes across his forehead. There was something different about that gappy smile: it was not yet manufactured.

'Do you know what I'd like?'

George followed my gaze, resting detached eyes on an image that would only serve to reinforce his failings day by day.

'I'd really like to see you play.'

'Don't be soft.'

'What's wrong with that?'

'You don't even like football.' He looked uncomfortable all of a sudden and I realised that the idea of watching himself was unbearable. 'And besides, I'm not going to start rooting around for a video; I've got no idea where Alex has put them. You know that we weren't allowed to have hair that long?' We were back to the photo. 'Or to take out our shin guards? At first, I stuck by all the rules; then I started breaking them.'

'You really weren't bad-looking, George.' He raised a sardonic eyebrow. 'I mean you still are, of course . . .'

He waved away my cajolery. 'I know what I am, and I know what I was. Just so that you know, I was never the poncy sort, not like these boy bands you see on the telly nowadays. I set the agenda: if I wore a leather jacket, leather jackets were in, if I stuck a bloody flower in my hair, blokes all over the world would do the same. I'm not joking . . .'

Inflamed by memories, vanity saturated his face for a moment. It drained away, leaving him regretful.

'But the only place I really felt I knew what I was doing

was on the pitch. Everything there came – I don't know – naturally.'

That explained the restlessness, the constant pacing and the sweet fixation: his body was no longer doing what it did best.

'When Manchester United signed me up,' he said, taking two sips of tea in quick succession, 'I couldn't believe that I was actually being paid to do something I loved. And then there were years when I could do no wrong. People wanted to know my views on everything: politics, aftershave, food, music and style – how crazy is that?'

I wondered at these sudden confidences, but a quick glance at his mug confirmed what I had begun to suspect: it was filled with an amber liquid.

'You were never really into the cars and Gucci suits, though, were you, George? Not like these Premier League guys now.'

'Oh, I've always liked a nice dinner jacket – and a nice motor,' he yawned. 'I can clean up pretty nicely when I want to, but some of these Italian labels I can't pronounce, let alone wear.' He looked down at his Ben Sherman Aertex, tattered jeans and slippers and we both laughed. 'No, the best thing about fame for me was always the women. Pretty girls and a nice vintage brandy.'

He gave up channel surfing, switched off the TV and turned towards me. The facetiousness in his eyes was blunted by tiredness and I felt a pang of sadness for him.

'Can't really beat those things. I've tried, and you can't.'

A pause as we both stared, inexplicably embarrassed, at the blank screen.

'Right, I'm going to turn in for the night. Shall I show

you your room? There are clean sheets and towels in there.'

Leading his way through the kitchen into a spare room, he pointed to a cupboard.

'Alex is, was, a house-proud little thing, so everything you need should be there. Bathroom's just here on the right. All set?'

There was just one thing.

'I couldn't borrow a T-shirt to sleep in, could I?'

'Course you could. Actually, I can do better than that.'

I watched his ankles, parched and cracked, climb the pine steps up to the master bedroom. A minute later he was back.

'Here, take these.' They were a pair of checked pyjamas, ironed and folded into a crisp square. 'They're mine. Given you're about twice my height, they might be a little snug,' he laughed, 'but they're comfy and clean.'

An inner wrangle was playing out across his features, and I thought I understood why. The situation − a young girl in his house, the sleeping arrangements and the pyjamas − all of it begged for flirtation. It was against his instincts to forego the chance of some pointed banter.

'George,' I began as we stood awkwardly at the door of my room. 'Thanks for letting me stay. I know the paper didn't exactly give you much choice and that the last thing you probably want right now is outsiders around, but I promise you won't even know I'm here.'

'That's doubtful, but actually,' he added, the words distorted by a yawn, 'I'm not sure I do mind. I'd be alone, wouldn't I, if you weren't here. And I don't fancy that much right now.'

With a gauche wave, he closed the door.

I lay rigid, listening to George's movements overhead until

94

eventually my eyes pulled themselves shut. Twenty minutes later, I was out of bed again, wedging a chair beneath the door handle. As I was doing it, the act felt juvenile and – oddly – like a betrayal. George did appear to be a different person in his own home. This new desire to share details of his past with me and explain his present motivations I had only glimpsed in Malta – yet there was no sign of any inclination to stop drinking. Phil had mentioned the acute homesickness George had suffered from – secretly and with shame – after being sent away to train aged fifteen at Old Trafford for two weeks. That homesickness, Phil maintained, had stayed with him all his life. Perhaps all he needed to get himself together was a period of calm at home.

But these, in retrospect, were the simplistic machinations of someone who didn't have a clue about alcoholism – or the man she was dealing with.

'Today,' I can still hear the significance George would invest in that word, 'today I am not going to drink.' That day was the first time I'd heard him say it, and I believed we'd made a breakthrough.

It was not yet eight, but sitting upright at the kitchen table in a blue tracksuit, wet hair combed back into a thirties-style slick, George was in a viciously optimistic mood.

'I'm going to go for a run, then at nine thirty,' he cleared his throat, balancing a triangle of toast on the edge of his plate, 'at nine thirty Cheryl is coming over.'

'Cheryl?'

'Alex's mum.' George disappeared beneath the table to tie his shoelace, so that his muffled voice reached me through layers of cherry wood. 'She's bringing the dogs back over.

Apparently Alex has flown off to Spain with some friends.'
His head resurfaced, spikes of hair now dislodged and falling across his eyes. 'The Costa del Sol. That's heartbreak for
you,' he added bitterly.

'Do you and her mum get on?'

'We're all right.' He paused, the positivity in his face
suspended for a moment. 'She and Alex's dad have been
pretty fantastic to me over the years, considering. They're
not happy about the way I've treated their daughter, obviously, and I haven't seen her since all that nonsense with that
piece-of-work from the pub – Paula – started. I'm guessing
she believed all the crap in the papers, but I don't know for
sure. Anyway,' he wandered out of the room, 'I'm off; I'll
try and stick it for an hour, so time me.'

Bracing himself for the sleepy circle of photographers
who, after nights spent in their cars, were drinking petrol
station coffee from polystyrene cups and smoking their first
cigarettes of the day, he opened the front door.

Judging by the displeasure radiating from her neat figure,
Cheryl wasn't about to forgive George his latest offences.
Her son-in-law was not yet back from his run, and she
was half an hour early. Our first meeting was difficult (the
combination of me being a journalist and a young woman,
I sensed, regrettable to say the least), and Cheryl's indig-
nant subtext – 'What does she think she's doing here in the
middle of a family crisis?' – as clear as it was understand-
able. Sitting across the table from one another, watching her
register that the striped shirt I was wearing belonged to her
son-in-law, we made hesitant small talk.

Along with the model looks she had passed on to her

daughter, life – or George – had leached a certain softness from her features. Beneath her blonde bob, Cheryl was assiduously made up, with the numbed quality of women used to dealing with family crises week on week.

The dogs had performed their duties well, prompting enough fuss to disguise the initial awkwardness. There had been the undoing of the leashes and affectionate scoldings; the expressions of admiration and the noisy doting from me. Bored of the charade, they had retreated to the rug by the fireplace. Now there was just the clicking of Cheryl's nails against the tabletop.

'I knew it was nonsense about you and George,' she said eventually, as though she had been weighing up whether or not to mention it for some time.

'I'm sorry?' I moved towards the kettle, and then instinctively drew back, lest the action be interpreted as infringing her domestic rights.

'In the paper. You know, "the mystery blonde".'

'Oh, that.' I wasn't sure whether I should apologise or not. 'I imagine you and Alex have seen your fair share of fiction printed over the years.'

'Oh, we have,' she exhaled, pulling mugs from cupboards and dropping teabags into them. 'Phil told us who you were, but even before then we knew there was nothing in those pictures.'

There was an uncomfortable silence as the kettle began to purr.

'Listen – Celia, isn't it? I know that you have a job to do. And I know how important it is for him to keep the column going throughout all this. But now really is a time when, as a family, we need to be left alone. If they're going to get through this, George and Alex need to work through their problems together.'

The kettle clicked itself off, giving out a protracted sigh of steam.

'This has been very hard on Alex, very hard. She has given her all to this marriage, and the two of them are still very much in love. But if there is any hope of saving it, the press really do need to give them their privacy.' She cleared up the tea things, calmly imposing order on the world around her, and I admired her self-control.

'I understand that, Cheryl, I do. I'm just here to babysit George until the media interest dies down a little and he gets his life back to normal ...'

Cheryl set her teacup down delicately, her mouth betraying the first signs of humour.

'Babysit? Perhaps we should have got him one of those a while ago. Seriously, though: you haven't known him long and I should tell you that there is no "normal" with George. That said, he's in a worse state now than he's ever been. And I don't know how much more acting out his body can take.' She paused, closed her eyes and shook her head. 'God, he's such a bloody fool. A bloody fool.'

Given the hysteria George tended to provoke, he was lucky to have someone like Cheryl around to soothe domestic temperaments. Yet something in the small, secret smile she was taking care to hide now reminded me of a similar expression on her daughter's face, when caught, at various dramatic points in her marriage, by the paparazzi. Both she and her daughter would have denied it forcefully, but I suspected a part of them did – even subconsciously – enjoy the public interest.

'So George says that Alex has gone off to the Costa del Sol?'

She nodded. 'Alex is lucky enough to have a fantastic support system in her friends, who knew that this was just what she needed to get some perspective. And I feel far happier knowing that she's away from all that lot,' she gestured towards the front door.

The skit of paws across the wooden floors and the cries of 'George!' from outside heralded her son-in-law's arrival. When was the last time George would have entered a room unnoticed, I wondered. When he was fifteen or sixteen? The door slammed shut.

'Cheryl?'

I got up to follow her next door, noting that she was visibly rearranging her features, smoothing them down like a dress in preparation for her part.

'George.' It was an admonishment more than a greeting.

Tacky with sweat, George was on his knees in an instant, immersing his face in ruffled neck fur. Sensing it was time to leave the two of them alone, I held out a hand to Cheryl.

'I'm going to do some reading in my room, give you two some space. Nice to meet you.'

'You too – and sorry if I appeared rude earlier. It's a difficult time.'

Lying on my bed, texting the office, I did my best to ignore the rising voices next door.

'What if I want to talk to her? To explain? Am I really not going to be allowed to do that?'

This was madness – and it had nothing to do with me.

With my hands over my ears, however, I could reduce Cheryl's words to an urgent female buzz. After what seemed like an extended lull, the front door slammed shut and the paparazzi, faithful spectators to this dramatic epic, started up their cries.

Aware that George might want to be left alone, and prematurely wearied by the violent mood changes he would work his way through following Cheryl's visit, I wondered whether now might finally be a good time to call home.

There was a knock at the door.

'Can I come in?'

I could see immediately that George had had a drink.

'So, that went well.'

We both laughed – him miserably, me with sympathy and a gaining unease.

'What did she say?'

He sank down on to the bed. 'Well, she won't let me have the dogs back, says she's going to keep them until I've "got myself together". Patronising bitch.'

I held my breath for a second.

'Sorry.' He looked up. 'Sorry. I shouldn't have said that.'

'That's OK.'

He was back to being a stranger, incalculable and in my room.

'Listen,' I moved a pile of towels off a chair in the corner and sat down as far from him as I could, 'why don't you write about your recovery plan in the paper this week, let people know all the stuff that you're doing right. Tomorrow the papers'll be full of pictures of you going for a jog with headlines like "George: Back on Track". You don't have to make any promises, but if you're upbeat and you make it clear that you're trying to turn over a new leaf, then Cheryl will hear about it and so will Alex ...'

'I like it,' he nodded sluggishly. 'That might be the only way to get through to Alex. Tell her that I'm back and persuade her to give me another chance. That ... Cheryl won't even give me her phone number out in Spain and her mobile is switched off.'

As a reader and a sentimentalist, George understood the power of words and was good at using his column to further his own personal aims. It amazed me how much self-criticism he would include in his writing ('I realise that I will need to change if I want our marriage to work') when there was so little of it in reality. It was the jocular self-deprecation which drew the public in: the random encounters with fans, doctors and women that he would recall in a way that reminded the public of his legendary status. Many of his 'confessions' were wild exaggerations. Some of them – unbeknown to everyone at the time – turned out to be lies. But they were lies he condoned using a child's rationale: because they were how he sincerely wished things could be.

Twice that morning, he had shuffled off into the kitchen with contrived excuses, the second time returning with a mug of what I knew to be white wine, and I was surprised by how offensive I found the subterfuge.

'George,' I said that afternoon, hoping there was no sign of reproach in my voice. 'Please.'

'Please what?'

'Just do me a favour. I'm not your wife or Cheryl – I don't care in the same way. I'm not going to freak out when you go on a bender, so don't bother lying about it.'

As I spoke, I questioned why this was true. From the start, it hadn't been the loss of control that had shocked me the most about George's addiction. Our drinking culture is such that we have all seen strangers in restaurants, work colleagues at office parties and aunts and uncles at family gatherings behave like strangers after drinking too much. Walking home at closing time conditions you to a certain amount of violence, too – but the Jekyll and Hyde effect and the fibs were impossible to get used to.

'Gee, your concern for my well-being is too much . . .'

'Well, I wish you wouldn't drink, obviously.' And I meant that. Later, I realised that like all the women who got close to him, part of me had been stupid enough to believe that I might be able to help. 'But why should that matter to you?'

Shame had long ago faded from his emotional chart – certainly where drink was concerned – but I thought I caught a touch of pique in the quick flicker of his eyelids.

'And look – it's your house,' I added with a rueful smile. 'So I'm in no position to say anything to you – you could sling me out on my ear if I did.'

'That I could – but not before I'd got my shirt back,' he smirked.

Although he seemed relieved, heading instantly to the kitchen for a refill, the realisation that there was no one there to beg him to stop drinking seemed to cause him a whole new malaise.

That day, he got steadily, evenly drunk, and I had to admit that in that state, George was the best company you could hope for. Funny and relaxed, the trembling of his hands and jowls would subside, the panic light in his eyes fading to a morose merriment. I believe now that his intelligence

– which had been obvious since our first meeting in Malta – was linked to his alcoholism. It made him want to see how far he could go in everything that he did.

Once his resolve had been broken, the whole day stretched before him joyously, a corresponding generosity of spirit flowering within him. Perhaps that explained why, for two people who scarcely knew one another, we'd quickly felt at ease. That afternoon we lay sprawled across the sofa watching a thriller, and while I sustained myself with tea and toast, George worked his way through Alex's Pinot Grigio. Just after six o'clock, with only those predictable, ever decreasing slices of sunlight to remind us of the outside world, his hand, wrapped around the remote control, once again began to shake and I realised that the alcohol must have run out.

The internal battle was brief but savage.

'I'm going to go down the offie,' he exhaled as casually as he could, half an hour later.

'You can't, George.' I paused, aware it sounded like an order. 'Honestly, you can't. If you go down there, there'll be pictures of you all over tomorrow's papers and it'll cancel out everything we've been trying to do.'

His eyes were glazed, arms crossed resolutely over his chest. 'Alex'll see them, she'll think everything you've been saying about turning over a new leaf is rubbish.' Which it was, of course. 'Do I really need to tell you why it's a bad idea? Jesus . . .' What did it matter to me if he got back together with his wife or not? 'Oh, look, do what you want, George.'

'I want a drink.'

And it occurred to me that his whole world, with its successes and failures, its peaks and troughs of joy and sadness, lay in that single sentence. Not 'another' drink, or even 'one more' – just a drink: pure, simple, and surely not that much to ask.

'You could go and get me one.' He had paused the thriller we were half-watching and was leaning forward now, spurred on by a plan. 'Nobody would know, and you could get a whole load of stuff while you're there. We need food anyway. The fridge is practically empty.'

He was pleading with me, and I guessed that he had used that same expression as a gap-toothed little boy, confident even then that few would say no to him.

'I can't do that; you know I can't buy you alcohol.'

He head-butted the air in a gesture of annoyance and we both sat in silence for a moment. A few minutes later, George disappeared upstairs to his bedroom and came back humming lightly.

'George?'

'What?'

Releasing the image of Morgan Freeman, frozen in his gun-toting stance on the screen, George sat back down. Half an hour later, the doorbell rang and a baseball-capped boy, visibly exhilarated from his encounter with the paparazzi outside, set down a large box of groceries just inside the front door.

'Thanks, mate – what do I owe you?'

Cackling devilishly, George handed the boy a folded note and sent him on his way.

Pushing aside the bread, Ritz crackers, two large bricks of cheddar and four bags of wine gums, he uncovered half a dozen bottles of South African Chardonnay. 'Get me some ice, would you?' I could hear George's dry swallows from where I was sitting, see him twisting his hands together with barely contained excitement.

'Get your own ice, George.'

But it was hard to stay angry: George's contentment was infectious. Nothing mattered to him at this point; he was unreachable and I envied him that state – so easily realised by alcohol.

Semi-anaesthetised, George finished his crossword before reaching for a book I had spotted in his hotel room in Malta. *The Dice Man* by Luke Rhinehart was a favourite he was reading for the tenth time. 'It's about a psychiatrist who makes these life-changing decisions based on the casting of the dice.' I could see why a book about a man who gambled with everything he had might appeal, and I wondered, aloud, whether those gambles paid off. 'I'll give it to you once I'm done and you'll see,' he promised, 'it really will change your life.' I'd thought the comment a little hyperbolic until months later, when I picked up a copy in a second-hand bookshop and noticed the tag line on the front of the book. 'This book will change your life' it shouted.

Looking back, it was during that short period at the barn that George began to seem real to me. His ability to fill the hours with conversation, pausing to snarl out quiz show answers at the TV ('The Four Gospels, you eejit – the Four Gospels!'), to entertain and teach me the sports-related trivia I was inexplicably becoming interested in, was turning him from a personality into a person. Although I missed my life and friends, my resentment of him, of the situation, was falling away. It took a colleague's rib, that afternoon, about Stockholm Syndrome to make me realise that I had stopped asking when I would be allowed to go home.

That day there hadn't been many photographers, although one or two would drop by occasionally on their rounds, peering brazenly in through the blinded windows, so that you could hear the cameras hanging from their necks tap like bird beaks against the glass. There was a permanent new fixture outside though: a good-looking, suited young reporter I recognised from the office, stationed in the driveway day and night.

'We thought you could do with a bit of extra support,' came the explanation; if I had any problems I should just give him a shout. Puzzled by this belated and, as I thought then, unnecessary chaperone, and failing to sense the obvious — that there was something being kept from me — I hadn't probed any further.

The lack of natural light was one thing I had found hard to bear. 'Don't you mind it?' I'd asked him.

'I'm used to it,' he'd replied. 'It seems funny to you, but I've had the blinds down everywhere I've lived for the past twenty years. My mum was like you,' he nodded. 'She used to hate it when I first became famous and people would stop and stare in at the windows of our house on the Cregagh Estate. I remember once, when I was kissing her goodbye, she said, "Don't take this the wrong way, George, but it's always a bit of a relief when you go, because we can put the blinds back up." '

That night, having heard him leave another insistent message for Alex, I braved a question I had wanted to ask for some time.

'Do you want her back, George?'

'I don't know.' He didn't look angry; just old, suddenly, and very sick. 'She used to say that we were soulmates – and I think she was probably right.'

Alex had taken over, he went on, but in a good way. She had forced him to see a doctor, sorted out his accounts and spring-cleaned his life so that it resembled what she wanted and not what it was. More than anything, she had given him a much-needed injection of hope.

'Those first few years together were some of the best of my life. She was so sure that everything was going to be all right – it sort of made me believe it too.'

After three years of AA, hypnotherapy, rehab and acupuncture, George had started drinking heavily again, disappearing for days on end – and the real fights had begun.

'People assume,' he told me with curious objectivity, 'that you slip into alcoholism, that it controls you. I don't know about other people, but I would make the decision. It was crystal clear to me what I was doing and every single thing that I was giving up when I did. Only the normal relative balance of things gets skewed in your head, so that your marriage or a contract worth hundreds of thousands of pounds in exchange for a glass of wine seems like a fair enough deal.'

Disillusioned by her husband and bored of the maternal role she had been cast in, Alex sought out compensation in designer dresses and celebrity parties.

'I guess she needed the attention I wasn't giving her any more. She was beautiful and young and wanted to show off in bars, at shop openings and in new restaurants. But I was bored of all that, and if she did drag me along I would just get drunk and embarrass her. Quite the life for a twenty-five-year-old girl.'

These self-deprecating footnotes were dotted about, there to ensure that my sympathies lay with him, and they worked. But despite my reluctant fondness for George, it was Alex I increasingly pitied: the disenchantment must have been savage.

'I wet the bed once,' George had volunteered with perverse pride, exploring my face for any signs of disgust. 'Can you imagine that? I wet the bed, like an old man, like an old bed-wetter.' He laughed but his laughter was noxious. 'I'd drunk a bottle of brandy before some awards ceremony we were going to, and downed everything I could get my hands on once we were there. The dinner went on for ever, and everyone was delighted to see me acting the way I was supposed to. Nothing disappoints the public more than me sober. But that night, when we got home and I went to lie down,' his throat dried up, 'I saw that I'd pissed myself. And I wasn't so far gone that I didn't think, "If only they could see George Best now".'

When he began to refer to himself in the third person, I knew that George had reached a zenith of drunken arrogance. I knew too that the genuine confidences had stopped. The first time it had happened, I had chided him for it, outraged by the realisation that, like a bad Hollywood film, he was trying to work me over. Then I gave up, more interested in the realisation that, in belonging to everyone, he had become detached from himself. George would talk about his childhood, his love affairs or his achievements on the pitch as though they were being viewed by an outsider – or had taken place in a separate lifetime. Past the self-consciousness of adolescence, it seemed so wrong to define yourself through the gaze of others, but that was what celebrity had done to him.

'So during all those years, even when it got really bad, you never cheated on Alex?'

'Never,' he maintained, his eyebrows insistent diagonals. 'Why would I? I loved her – and I've had a lot of women in my life.' There was that boastful twitch at the corners of his mouth again. 'Although it did take me some time to get the whole courting thing right.'

I laughed. 'What does that mean?'

'I was quite shy as a young boy. Mostly, I'd have to have a drink just to get the courage up to talk to a girl, and that carried on well into my first days at Man U.' He took a sip of wine and rubbed his eye with a cracked knuckle. 'Pulling girls, when we were away for a game, was a spectator sport for us. You'd be judged on how well you did – and by that I mean quantity, not quality – and I'd often find myself pulling uglier and uglier birds as the evening wore on, just to make up the numbers.'

Later it became a kind of whimsical game; like the clothes and the cars, a testing of his godlike powers. 'I would deliberately go for the most unattainable women: the beauty queens, the best friends, the mothers, anyone who had a reason not to get involved with me – just to see if I really could have anyone I wanted. Women had become a game to me and I wanted to be better at it than anyone else.'

His smile faded.

'But you know what I always thought? That some of the normal girls – shop girls and the like – some of them were far more stunning than the big stars. Part of it was maybe that you never felt you could reach those pin-ups, even when you were lying next to them in bed, so that there was something, I don't know, *unreal* about the whole thing.'

I looked through a chink in the blinds at our stoic guard, noting with a fleeting sense of regret that the perfect August day we had missed was turning into a perfect August night, all moonstone shadows and grass-scented breezes. A friend, not knowing that I was still caught up in this assignment, had sent a text message inviting me to join a group of people at the pub and I pictured them all outside in the beer garden, sending each other off to buy rounds.

'Great big blonde Viking women,' he was still running though his conquests, shaking his head like a dog caught in a frenzy of sensuality. 'I couldn't get enough of them.'

'Didn't it detract from the fun, knowing that a lot of it was about "sleeping with George Best"? Or is that just not something a man would worry about?'

Mildly shocked, he pinched my side. 'Hey – what are you implying? That they were after the fame, rather than me?'

'Oh, I'm sorry – how embarrassing,' I flung back. 'You thought it was all about your sizzling personality, didn't you?'

But he was serious. 'Things were different then.' He gestured towards the closed blinds, glowing caramel in the descending sunlight. 'Or maybe not, maybe you're right.' Releasing his limbs from a long, shuddered stretch, he turned to face me. 'Though there weren't so many "My Sex Romps with Best"-style headlines in those days, for some reason.'

There was a silence, and I hoped I hadn't sparked a bout of morbid introspection.

'Help me out here, George, what does a romp actually involve?'

'A romp?' He scratched his beard. 'A romp is when I tear around a house or hotel room in wild pursuit of a girl, both of us wearing very little. They tend to end on the floor – not necessarily in the bedroom – and there's usually a fair amount of giggling involved.'

Half an hour later, enfeebled with laughter at the wild claims of George's 'hat tricks in the bedroom', we coasted along on the aftermath of our shared mirth until George, his eyes still pearled with tears, started up again.

'I'd love to be able to confirm all the stories, of course, but my memories usually stop after the four bottles of champagne and room service club sandwich. Still, I'm grateful for the references, and actually,' there was that bragging jut of the chin again, 'I could always manage it, even when I'd had a skinful.'

There was inevitably a moment, I was learning, when George turned from skilful entertainer to lubricious boozer. But I no longer felt threatened when George's seduction routine – the flattery, personal questions and wandering hands – started up. It was briefer and less enthusiastic than that first night, with a perfunctory, dutiful feel to it, and he was easily rebuffed with a laugh or a joke.

'So, George,' I resumed, 'in order of preference: drink, women, football.'

He laughed. 'That's easy: women, drink, football.' His forehead corrugated into an even series of lines. 'No, that's wrong: football, women, drink.' A sigh of frustration. 'No, that's wrong too. It depends when you mean, Trouble. When I was growing up it was the booze; back then the booze was a way to get to the girls. Then the girls were replaced by the booze.'

'And where's the football in all this?' I asked, amused by how earnestly he was tackling the question.

'The football?' he took a sip of wine, swilled it around like mouthwash and swallowed noisily. 'The football was always there.'

I knew that there had been a shift – a progression, even – in our relationship, blooming now with the artificial intensity of a hothouse flower, when George began to probe more deeply into my personal life. One of the least civilised traits of most famous people I have met since is their unapologetic lack of interest in others, but George's natural curiosity had somehow resisted being quashed. Yes, he could talk about himself tirelessly, but that was partly a reaction to the weight others had for years placed on his every word. Every conversation was a series of questions to him; every answer a present to hand out or deny.

'I've told you before – there's nobody at the moment,' I had protested when he pressed me on the subject of my love life.

'Not even some spotty young reporter at the office?'

'Not even a spotty young reporter. I'm too busy hanging out with loonies like you to meet anyone.'

Disregarding the insult, George frowned. 'Well, I hope you do find someone. Because in my view you're quite a little lady.'

He stood awkwardly by the sofa for a moment, looking down at me with a lopsided smile, the kind that forms organically, not through any desire to impress a frame of mind, false or otherwise. I imagined the different incarnations of that smile: the one he gave his mother, and the one he used to win over all those women years later. Lazy in its lilt, grating in its confidence, it was one I have recognised in lotharios ever since: special, to the extent that it pretended to hand the power over to you. *I could tame him,* they must all have thought.

I yawned.

'You going to bed?'

'Yes.'

'Really?'

'Yes.'

'Need any . . .'

'Goodnight, George.'

That night, I wedged the chair back beneath the door handle.

I should have guessed that the idyll of those forty-eight hours wouldn't last. With so much threatening to upset the balance we had precariously constructed, I'm amazed it didn't collapse sooner.

Twice I had knocked on George's door the following morning, a cup of tea in my hand, and received no answer. When I pushed the door open an inch or two, I saw at once that something was wrong. Perched on the end of the bed in a dressing gown which fell open to reveal slender legs, their tan failing to hide the mottled bruising on the shins (a consequence of the medication, he'd told me), George was in a stupefied state. On the floor, in between his parted legs, was a bottle of Pinot Grigio, and in the hand hanging limply from his knee, a newspaper.

Watching a man uncork a bottle of wine before eleven in the morning would once have shocked me; very quickly, it had become acceptable: a part of George's consistent excess. I knew from George that Alex would try to feed him as much as possible early in the day, because after the first glass, there would be little eaten besides the sweets he needed to keep his yo-yoing blood sugar levels in check. This morning, it wasn't yet ten and the bottle was half empty.

'George?' I clicked my fingers in front of his face. 'Hey. Everything OK?'

He glanced from me to the paper in his hand, then threw it, as if it were tainted, on the bed.

'Some helpful sod put that through the letterbox this morning. It's Alex. She's been mouthing off to a reporter in Spain, saying she can't trust me any more, calling me a lying bastard. And you know what the worst thing is? This is your paper – *my* paper, I should say. So much for loyalty.'

An idea jolted him out of his monotone.

'Did you know about this? Did the paper tell you that your colleagues were hunting down my wife for an exclusive?'

I saw no point in lying. 'I knew we had people out there, but I didn't know they'd managed to get hold of her.' I waited for a reaction, but his face was blank. 'Is it all lies?' I asked gently.

'No,' he shook his head. 'That's the worst of it. It's pretty much all true.'

'I'm sorry.' Getting up strenuously, he reached for a used wine glass on the windowsill and waved the bottle around. 'Would you care for . . . ?'

'I'm all right, thanks, George.'

'Oh. OK.' Disregarding the glass on the bed, he sank down with a heavy crunch.

'Jesus, George.'

Pulling his hand out from beneath him he examined it with disinterest. The glass had sliced through the smooth skin inside his forearm, and blood – thin, purplish, ill-looking – was slipping easily, thin as water, down his arm into the groove of his hand.

'Oh God, George, give it here.'

Pulling him through to the bathroom, I tried to stem the blood which, because of his defunct immune system, now refused to clot. Through the toilet roll wrapped around his arm, a redcurrant stain was already seeping through.

'That's enough!' he lashed out. 'Just get off me, you bitch.'

I felt my stomach jolt, like when you miss a step, at the insult. For the first time since I'd first arrived at the barn, I felt scared.

As his eyes scanned the floor of the bedroom for his wine bottle, I tried to rationalise myself calm again. In a minute he would revert back to being the crossword obsessive who lent me his pyjamas, but something had closed down inside me. What did the rest matter when he could behave like this?

When I spoke, the sound of my own fear mortified me. 'What are you looking for, George?'

Gripping me by the shoulders, he moved his face to within an inch of mine – and smiled. 'The wine. Where have you put the wine?'

'It's there,' I pointed to the bottle, discarded on a side table.

Letting go of me, he seized it by the neck, a tatter of toilet roll hanging from his hand and forearm, put the bottle to his

mouth and drank. Lids closed and fluttering with contentment like those of a sated baby, he kept on drinking, small
drops escaping the corners of his mouth and trickling on to
the lapels of his shirt. By the time he put the bottle down,
the level was so diminished that he observed it with astonishment and a mild conceit, before swivelling around to face
me again.

'You still here?' The words were garbled by fluid in his
throat, and I could see him fighting the spasms in his stomach.
'Yes.'

'Read to the end of the article – go on! She's got a new
career planned out on telly,' he spat the word out. 'A whole
new life planned out without me.'

Although I couldn't see his face, I thought I could hear
tears in his voice. But after the way he had spoken to me
earlier, I found his self-pity pathetic rather than touching.
This was all his fault; no wonder it was so unbearable to
him.

'There's nothing in there about divorce, George,' I said
coolly as I got up. 'And she doesn't rule out the possibility
that you two might get back together – though God knows
how much she'd have to love you to do that.'

On the way downstairs, I thought of the things I could
have said to placate him. I could have told him that people
never realise how much they say in interviews, and that
Alex might well call at some point and apologise for the
more barbed comments – but I didn't feel inclined to lessen
his pain, and by five o'clock, there had been no news from
Alex.

To make matters worse, a belligerent phone call to Cheryl
had revealed that his wife was back in the country.

'So, when's this television career kicking off then?' he jeered into the receiver, pacing from the sitting room to the kitchen, where he filled up his glass, and back again. 'First I've heard of any of it. Nope, that's right, Cheryl, she never mentioned a thing about it to me. Turns out there's a lot about my wife I didn't know. Got a new boyfriend too, has she? Someone out in Spain? Shame nobody thought to tell good old George any of this . . .'

I had tried to dissuade him from making the call, knowing the ructions his paranoia would cause. Feeling I had lost control of the situation, I began to wonder whether I should call Phil.

Letting herself in with her daughter's key, Cheryl looked from George's sulky shape on the sofa, a fresh bottle jammed in between his thighs, to me, at the window. Without waiting for either one of us to acknowledge her presence she moved briskly through the room and pulled the bottle from her son-in-law's lap.

'Right: up you get. None of this is going to help.'

Breaking from his coma, he leered up at her. 'Well, look who it is.'

'I don't know what's gone on between you and Alex, but understand this, George: I will always believe my daughter. If you really think you two have a chance, after all this, then you need to make an effort because this'll be your last one.'

She was brave to tackle him in the state he was in.

'A chance?' Indignation propelled him out of his seat into a threatening stance. 'How's that going to happen when your daughter won't answer her phone and seems happy to talk to every journalist in town, but not her husband?'

'I won't be spoken to like that,' Cheryl replied evenly, clearly accustomed to such scenes. 'I shall tell Alex that nothing has changed.'

'You do that,' sneered George. 'Your daughter's not welcome here any more either. So you can give me back her keys right now. Oh, and tell her she can see the dogs on weekends if she likes.'

George got up and walked threateningly towards Cheryl, but she was uncowed.

'Don't you dare threaten me.' That staunch middle-class accent showed no signs of cracking. 'If it weren't for my daughter turning your life around you'd already be dead. She saved you, and this is the thanks she gets?'

'Just get out.' George knew that he had lost. 'Don't bother with the keys – tell Alex I'll have the locks changed.'

'You do that,' she flung back as she marched out of the door, outside which a cluster of snappers, scenting a domestic scene, had reconvened.

George didn't say a word, turning his back on me and heading into the kitchen for more wine. Only when he left the room did I hear the drill of my mobile phone on the table: Phil.

'Hello?' Then, without waiting for a reply he continued, 'We have a problem.'

'Yes, we do,' I sank down on the sofa, relieved someone, Cheryl perhaps, had filled him in.

'No, no . . .'

There was a hum of motorway in the distance.

'Where are you?'

'I'm on my way to you.'

A second influx of relief.

'Good – I didn't want to call you but ...'

'... And so is Alex. She just rang me. Apparently her mother's just had a bust-up on the phone with George, who's completely lost it.'

'She's just been round here.'

'Oh Jesus. Why didn't you tell me that he was getting this bad?'

'I was going to but I ...'

'Anyway, with any luck I'll get there before Alex does. What kind of a state is he in?'

I felt a buck of annoyance at the divine pronoun; at the amount of people whose plans and moods revolved around George's drinking.

'Bad. He's just gone up to the bedroom with a bottle now. I'm not sure how much alcohol there is in the house, actually, so ...'

The line cut off for a moment, Phil's voice drifting back to me mid-sentence a second later: '... stashes everywhere. I once found a bottle of brandy in the bathroom cabinet so trust me, there will be plenty in the house. Anyway,' he was firm, 'it's not your job to try and stop him. I can't and I've known him a lot longer than you have. Just hang tight. I'll be there in twenty.'

He was too late, although at the stage George had reached, no amount of prepping would have helped. He had been locked in his bedroom since Cheryl's departure, and I had been forced to warn him through the door of Alex's imminent arrival.

The door opened slowly. 'When will she be here?'

'Any minute now, I think.'

He held himself up by the doorframe. 'What does she want?'

'I have no idea.'

A pause.

'I'd better clean myself up then.'

My first impression of Alex – amidst the clicks and wheezes of the cameras – was a flash of honey blonde and deep bronze.

I had been watching the news when she let herself into the barn, disappearing into the kitchen where George was waiting, wearing brown suede shoes I'd never seen before, hair still wet from the ice-cold shower he'd taken, a second cup of strong coffee in his hands. A minute later, when she strode up the stairs two at a time with George close behind, I caught a closer look: gym-chiselled legs in jeans shorts, the shadowy groove of her lower back visible beneath a short white T-shirt.

'You look good. Thin, but good; are you eating?'

The door was ajar and I could hear every word.

'I've come to get some clothes, George – not to talk.'

She had her mother's clear, polite speech and it occurred to me that perhaps all along it had been her, not him, who was in control of the marriage.

'I know that, but Al . . .'

The door closed and I stared blindly at the pages of my book until I heard Phil pull up outside.

'Well, that didn't take them long,' he said, giving me a kiss on the cheek and a frazzled smile.

'The paps? There weren't any earlier – now suddenly they're all back.'

Phil crashed down into an armchair.

'What about you, eh? You coping all right? Bet this is turning out to be one of the weirder jobs you've been on.'

'The weirdest,' I confirmed with a smile, holding back, 'and the first'.

A burst of words from above, like somebody turning a recording of George's voice on and off, silenced us.

'How long have they been up there?'

'About fifteen minutes.'

'Humph.'

Picking up one of George's quiz books from the table and splicing it open with a thumb, he began to flick through the pages.

'He rings me, you know, and there's no "Hi Phil, what are you up to?" Just straight away the question.' He began to read one out: 'In which country would you find the rivers Oder and Vistula?'

'Give me a hint.'

As I spoke a female voice, edging on hysteria even through the walls, drowned me out. 'How many times do we have to go through this, George? You're not listening to me.'

'Poland,' continued Phil, without so much as a flinch. 'Let's try another one: where in the human body would you find the Islets of Langerhans?'

I looked at him, incredulous. These volatile situations had clearly long ago ceased to affect him. A week in George's company had left me nervy and exhausted – how could he still be here, still devoted, still loyal after thirty years?

'You listening? Where in the human body would you . . .'

I got up, feeling like an involuntary voyeur. I needed to go home.

'I can't, Phil.'

Holding my gaze, he went on, 'George's sister told me that once during a family lunch in a pub in North London, nobody could get the answer to one of the quiz questions in one of the Sunday papers. George got up, hailed a cab and went all the way back to his Cheyne Walk flat to check the answer in the encyclopaedia. Apparently he made the cabbie wait outside, and then got him to drive him back to the pub. The fare was over fifty quid.'

I laughed despite myself, a laugh ending in a hard kick of resentment. Those stupid quizzes, the way George's right eye slouched shut when he was being cheeky, the way he called me Trouble when it was quite clearly not me but him who caused trouble of epic proportions; and the stories – those constant ghostly snapshots of George – had me caught up in a way I hadn't expected.

'Do you know what the worst thing is, Phil? That although none of this is my business, I've actually started to worry about him – can you believe that?' I tried to shake my hands – tightly knotted around one another – free, but exasperation had locked the joints tight.

'Yes, I can,' Phil's mouth trickled into a smile. 'You wouldn't be human if you were able to spend more than a couple of days with George and not like him. I've seen men and women fall under his spell in under an hour.' He cocked his head to one side. 'Now, that's when he's on form, of course . . .'

That irritated me too – I wasn't some fan.

'That's the worst of it: I keep hearing him being talked about like a god; it's as though we should all be honoured to be near him.'

Phil waved a hand through the air to silence me. 'You've never seen him play, have you?'

We were interrupted by a sob from the bedroom and the slam of a cupboard door. 'Don't you dare bring that up now ...'

'No. I tried to get him to show me an old game the other day but he didn't seem too keen.' Suddenly, dreading the idea that I would be immune to George's genius, I didn't want to see him play any more.

But Phil was already on his hands and knees, dislodging a pile of videos from behind the television.

'Alex is like you, says the beautiful game basically leaves her cold. That, I can believe, but watching George play won't.'

'Honestly, Phil,' I attempted. 'Don't worry. Of course I get that he was this incredible player. The one,' I went for a stock sporting hyperbole, 'who took football from the back to the front pages. I do get that.'

'All that talk's bollocks if you haven't seen him in action,' retorted Phil, pausing in his search to balance the remainder of his cigarette on the side of the ashtray. 'But you'll see what he's all about in a second. Aha – here it is.'

The cigarette burned, forgotten, down to a stub, leaving a saffron stain on the porcelain as Phil busied himself with the machine. Finally, he sat back and pressed play.

'George always used to say that football was like show business as far as he was concerned, and, Christ, I do sometimes think the man should have been an actor. So you don't have to,' he donned a petulant female whine, '*get football* to appreciate the full glory of him.'

He followed my gaze to the closed door upstairs. 'They may be up there some time,' he chuckled. 'Relax.'

123

An anaemic pitch, Windsor Park according to the ticker line, filled the screen; dots of green, white and yellow zigzagging up and down it like a moving Impressionist landscape.

'Right. Here it comes . . . I can't believe he hasn't shown you these. It used to be that you couldn't stop him talking about the hat tricks, the way he used to humiliate one defender after another, ripping victory out of the other team's hands at the ninetieth minute – but these days it's like he doesn't enjoy talking about it any more.'

'Maybe it makes him sad,' I ventured, looking over at the trophies, shiny and impassive on their table, and wondering whether it was as personal a tragedy to George as a beautiful woman getting old.

I recognised him immediately. Something about the boyish slope of those shoulders and slender legs exuded a grace he still half-possessed today. I had expected to be deafened by the cacophony of the game: the thunder of feet, a violent cavalcade of bodies as they advanced towards the goal, but George's feet hardly touched the ground. He was like a ballet dancer, weaving in and out of the other players – carthorses in comparison – flaunting that effortless dexterity. And when the camera panned in on his sideburned face, the wind sweeping his long hair from it, the purity of his expression stunned me.

'Just look at him,' Phil paused the image just as, having flicked the ball away from England goalkeeper Gordon Banks and headed it into the net, George ran towards the crowd, drinking in their adoration.

'Do you know that they disallowed that goal? Criminal, that was.' He paused. 'Nimble little fella, wasn't he?

"Nijinsky-like", they'd call him. He used to get sick a lot, and he was always shyer than the rest, but within the team he had the reputation of being the one with the gift of the gab. And pretty quick he learned to play up to that. I always think that a footballer's life,' he leaned forward in his chair, tapping his cigarette on the table, 'is made up of highs and lows; celebration and commiseration – that's all George knew for years. And when he wasn't drunk,' he looked up at me, 'he was drinking.'

Alex appeared, dragging a large leather bag down the stairs behind her.

'Do you have to let him smoke in here, George?' Alex asked when she got her breath back. "Still, I guess you're in no position to lecture people on their lives, are you?'

'I've always let Phil smoke in here. Why are you being like this?' I could hear the words catch in his throat, hoarse from arguing. 'Why are you being such a cow?'

'You just can't help yourself, can you?' This was said without anger – just sadness. 'Mum told me what you said to her. I would have hoped you'd have more respect after everything she and Dad have done for you . . .'

She stopped short, aware for the first time of my existence.

'You're the journalist, right? Don't take this the wrong way, but what are you doing in my house?'

I tried to formulate an answer, one that would be both sensitive and pragmatic, but she had turned back to George, now flanked by Phil, who was trying, ambitiously, to placate both parties at once.

I was pleased at the deflection: it gave me an opportunity to observe the woman George had told me, in wildly fluctuating terms, so much about.

Get to know one half of a couple first, and the other always comes as a surprise. Superficially, George and Alex's connection wasn't hard to understand. Sculpted and symmetrical beneath the perfect circumflexes of her eyebrows, Alex's face worked in symphony with her athletic body: it exuded a kind of smouldering vitality which suited strong emotion. It was a face which photographed well and had been photographed often, but which, through the sheer frequency of giving up that image, had forfeited something – some natural sweetness, perhaps. There was too much cynicism in her eyes for a woman as young as she was, and I felt for her.

'Alex, please,' George was pleading now, trying to prise the bag's handles from her grip.

'Alex, love, you know he can come through this.' It was Phil's turn to try. 'He has before; he'll do it again.'

But she was shaking her head, eyes downcast.

'I think of all the chances I've given you, George, all the times I've said . . .' Squeezing shut lashes heavy with mascara, she allowed a gurgle of frustration to escape. 'No, no, no. I've had it. I told you that in Malta. And you can change the locks for all I care, do whatever you want. We'll see what the lawyers have to say.'

With that she turned, threw open the front door and, in full view of the photographers outside, whipped around to face George again.

'Actually,' she pulled something from her handbag, something small that caught the light, and held it in the palm of her hand.

'Here – just take it. Take it, George.'

Had Alex intended the 'key handover' to be caught on

camera? If that had been her plan, and I had no reason to suppose that it was, it was carried out with a slickness that was both admirable and ever so slightly chilling.

CHAPTER FIVE

SLUMPED AGAINST THE SIDEBOARD in the kitchen, head bowed, George took a swig from the bottle of cooking brandy beside him.

'We ran out of wine, Trouble. Any idea how that happened? 'Cause,' he slurred, 'a real sitter, a good sitter, would never let that happen.'

He attempted a comedic roll of the eyes in my direction, which failed, coming off as barmy.

'George.'

How did Phil stay so calm? I knew that however many and varied the scenes he had witnessed were, he still felt the implications of George's dramas deeply, yet rather than give in to hysteria, he always reacted with 'how can we fix it' logic.

'George! Hey, mate, put that down a second. Talk to me. Let's thrash out a game plan.'

No reaction. George hadn't even registered his friend's words.

'Mate, come on. We knew she wasn't going to be easy on you. But you know, in the piece, she says nothing about divorce,' he brushed an imaginary piece of lint from his trouser leg. 'I think she just wanted you to see what she's been living through in black and white: give you a kick up the ...'

He stopped when, like me, he saw that a series of muscular contractions were causing George's abdominals to heave in and out, working their way up into his throat with the unnatural machinations of a sick cat. Before either one of us had time to act, George began to vomit, noisily and without embarrassment. The first reflux just missed the sink, sliding, a watery salmon liquid, down the white-panelled cupboards and on to the floor.

'George, what have ...' I began, but of course it was blood.

'It happens,' Phil explained later, while George was cleaning himself up in the bathroom. 'His stomach's eaten away from the alcohol, so after a binge ... You must have noticed the smell.'

I had – a sour heat, like sweat but stronger – but through some misplaced attempt at politeness, I shook my head.

'You must have. I asked the doctors when I first noticed it. Honestly, I couldn't work out what it was.' Clearing his throat, he started again, and I could see that beneath the can-do attitude there was only the interminable torment of watching his best friend die. 'So I asked the doctors and they said that it was because George was rotting inside. They gave it some fancy name, of course, but when I asked what it meant, they explained it like that: said that he was rotting inside.'

For a moment neither of us said a thing. I had forgotten the office or how badly I wanted to escape this story; I knew only that George had to be taken somewhere where he could be looked after.

'The Priory – do you reckon we could convince George to go there?'

Reaching for his Silk Cuts, rethinking it, and slipping the pack back into his pocket, he shook his head. 'No way. The only place he'll go voluntarily is a health farm in Liphook, Forest Mere, owned by a mate of his called Stephen Purdew. He and Stephen have known each other for over twenty years and he's stayed there dozens of times. Tony Adams set up a clinic in the grounds that specialises in rehabilitating sports stars, but George has always refused to see any of the counsellors there. They do serve alcohol at Forest Mere, but Stephen keeps a very close eye on George and makes sure he's looked after. If we can get him down there, there's a chance he might snap out of this.'

When Phil came out of the bathroom with George, after ten minutes of low-level discussion, they both looked relieved.

'How did you manage it?' I whispered, as George meekly began to put together a bag of clothes.

'Alex,' he said, throwing George's wash things into a bag. 'I told him it was the only way she'd have him back – which is already a big if. Now listen, there's a window in the sitting room overlooking the back garden. Why don't you get your stuff together and I'll unlock it. If we slip out that way, we have a chance of getting down to Forest Mere without being seen.' A pause. 'I'm guessing that would suit your purposes too?'

He was right. Did we really want George photographed stumbling from his house, dazed, with a blood-stained shirt and bandaged wrist? Far better to give the paper time to decide on which version of events to print. The rehab development, though undoubtedly what George needed, did create one concern: once there, would he want to cut himself off from the outside world – and me? How was this going to work?

'I'm sure they'll put you up in a room near his,' said Phil, reading my mind.

'Good. I'm guessing the paper will want George to write about why he's decided to check in there. Make sure people know that it's *his* decision.'

Clownish with drink, George clambered out of the window, catching his shin on the sash as he went and swearing under his breath. It brought back our backstairs escape from Malta, with George in a similar state, and I wondered why I wasn't angry with him now, as I had been then. Perhaps it was because none of his troubles had seemed real to me back then. It takes time and effort to feel sympathy for the people whose lives play out on a public stage; sometimes it's impossible to believe that anything can affect them in the same human sense as the rest of us. I hadn't understood the weight of George's demons before, believing them to be self-indulgence. Nor did I conceive at the start that his attachment to Alex might be as strong as it was – more so, that he might depend on her. If this really was it for Alex and George, his disintegration would be fast. Who would take him on now?

Phil had had the presence of mind to park his car in a lane a few minutes' walk away, so the three of us stole, like inept burglars, through back gardens, glancing in at families frozen before their TV screens, until we reached it. Speeding out unseen on to the motorway, with the radio so low that the presenter's voice rose and fell in wafts of sentimentality, George fell asleep. Occasionally a street lamp would light up his face, colouring his cheekbones a violent yellow and deepening the hollows like a skull. Phil, meanwhile, eyes fixed on the road ahead, had the absent quality of a man who knows he should be elsewhere. I looked from him to George, who was lolling in jolting degrees towards my shoulder, and wondered at the casual harm he inflicted on everyone who loved him.

Before leaving, I had rung the office to set out George's plans.

'I want you in there keeping an eye on him,' my boss had ordered. 'It would be good to get a few positive headlines at this point.'

'My Road to Recovery'? I heard myself suggest, and it struck me, not for the first time, that the tone we journalists adopt can be horribly flip. Several times, over the course of my career, I've caught myself skimming over the surface of a subject's life, without pausing to reflect on the realities of their joys and suffering. Yet it was true that something about George's disintegration mesmerised people. Which would sell more papers, I wondered: his redemption or his failure?

Oblivious to my thoughts and Phil's quiet suffering, George gave a moist yawn, curled his feet up on the back seat and, as though it was the most natural thing in the world, laid his head on my lap. A sense of protectiveness coupled with distaste kept me rigid until our breathing gradually synchronised and I too fell asleep. We awoke within minutes of each other, just over an hour later, as we passed a discreet sign to the Forest Mere Health Farm. Two miles

132

to go. As I struggled to focus, George's eyes began to blink themselves awake.

'Nothing changes, does it?' he murmured, his intonations feminine with sleep.

I looked down at him.

'I came here a couple of months before the transplant, without knowing how sick I was. I was just going through the motions, you know? Trying to keep everyone happy. I left after a week, and started drinking heavily again straight-away. It was around that time that I began to get these terrible pains in my gut.' He shifted on to his side, so that his cheek lay more comfortably against my thigh, muffling his speech a little. 'I'd be walking the dogs or going for a run and suddenly find myself doubled up on the floor. I tried to hide it from Alex; I knew she'd make me go to the hospital, and I guessed, of course, what they would tell me: that I had cirrhosis of the liver. But one day, Alex came home from her mum's to find me collapsed on the bathroom floor. I didn't even have the strength to argue, so she called an ambulance and when we got to the hospital it felt like giving myself up to the police – sort of a relief, too. Isn't that weird?'

'No,' I shook my head, and it felt strange, not unpleasant, to be providing reassurance. 'You can't keep up that old pace, George. Maybe it's OK to let yourself off the hook about that.'

'I remember once,' he cleared the rumble of laughter from his throat, 'when I was eight, I stole a pound from my mum's purse, and it was such a relief when she found out. That was exactly how I felt at the hospital. At least it was all over, you know? I knew that the thing I had dreaded the most was going to happen: they would tell me I had to stop drinking.'

Hazy platitudes from well-worn love songs had dissolved into silence, and I wondered whether Phil had deliberately turned off the radio in order to listen in on what George was saying.

'They put me in a room while Alex went outside to talk to the doctors.' He seemed to be talking to himself now more than me. 'And there was a mirror by the bed. God knows why 'cause I'm guessing the sick don't usually like to look at themselves – but I picked it up. My skin,' his breathing quickened and he reached up to touch his face with his fingertips, 'it was yellow – I mean *really* yellow. I could have auditioned for a part in *The Simpsons*. My cheeks and eyes had swollen up, though not much more than they are now, I suppose, and I looked about a hundred and two. The doctor told me straight: one more drink would kill me. But once the Antabuse tablets were sewn into my stomach lining, he told me that I wouldn't even be able to keep that one drink down, so I would be OK. Two things went through my head.' He looked up at me. 'That he was right. And that the tablets wouldn't work for me, because it would be sod's law that I would be the only person in the world who could get away with it.'

He held a kind of pride, I realised, in his own body's defiance of all things medical, as though this confirmed that he was right to be drinking. And there was the more obvious pleasure of proving the doctors wrong.

'Dead, they said,' he added with a bluster that made me flinch. 'And I'm still going. It was funny though, just before the operation, after the doctor had given me the anaesthetic and I was waiting to go under, I had this really strong déjà-vu back to my birthday, a few years back, in that great Mayfair Casino …'

'The Palm Beach,' came Phil's voice from the front.

'The Palm Beach, that's right – that joint was something special. Phil and I have spent many a good night there, but that night they'd really looked after us. I don't think we paid for a single drink. I remember thinking that life couldn't get much better than that.'

'The Palm Beach Casino,' murmured Phil again, lingering over the words. 'We had some good times there.'

Pulling himself up off my lap and stretching his neck right and then left, George stared out of the window.

'People said I didn't deserve to have a second chance after the way I'd behaved. They said it was "outrageous", as if I hadn't realised what a gift of life that transplant was.' A pause. 'But I am fairly outrageous, I suppose.'

I laughed. 'That you are, George … that you certainly are.'

I didn't see the beauty of Forest Mere – the elegance of that Edwardian building with its annexes, rambling gardens and, in the midst of it all, the serenity of that lake – until the following morning. That night, the welcome sign, trees, and building beyond were lost in frittered shades of orange and black. Around the electric gates, shielding their eyes from the headlights, great huddles of paparazzi rose like furies from the ground: they had got there before us.

'Mr Best!'

'George! Give us a pic!'

'Wanker!'

George was wise to that paparazzi ruse – abusing a celebrity to get them to turn around – but this time his instincts took over and he put his face to the window. Realising his mistake immediately, he doubled over in his seat. A few seconds later, we were through, but the suddenness of his movement had left him in discomfort.

'You OK?'

'No. I don't think I am, mate.' His arms were folded tightly around his stomach. 'It's playing up again . . .'

'Will he be able to see a doctor tonight, Phil?' I whispered, leaning in towards him.

'It's all taken care of. Don't you worry about it. Now, I'm not staying,' he added quietly.

'You're what?'

Phil ignored him: 'You should try to get an early night while I'll settle him in tonight.'

'Can you two stop talking about me as though I'm not here?'

'And I'll be at the end of the line and back to check in on you both in a couple of days' time, OK?'

I could have done with Phil there the following morning, when, as we made our way downstairs to breakfast, a man shook George's hand, adding ingratiatingly, 'And I don't believe a word of what your wife's saying about you in today's paper. I, for one, am proud to say I've met you.'

A visit to the health farm's boutique enlightened us. Another tabloid had got hold of Alex and this interview made the previous one look like a love letter.

In 'My Eight-Year Ordeal' – illustrated by a picture of Alex looking both seductive and victimised – she had categorically declared the marriage over, claiming her husband was 'a madman' who had thrown curry in her face, hacked off her hair while she slept and covered her body in black marker pen. It was highly possible, I concluded, that she had discovered some new misdemeanour George had committed. After all, what purpose – aside revenge – could it possibly serve to share all this with the public? Still, these lucrative confessionals had become the natural fallout from most celebrity break-ups, and while I couldn't understand why Alex had chosen to do this, I certainly didn't blame her.

Like the enhanced functions advertised on a box of laundry detergent, George's offences were broken down into a neat series of bullet points at the start of the article. George was silent as, back in his room and sitting side by side on his bed, we worked our way through the piece together. One line stood out and I froze as I read it: on her twenty-fifth birthday, Alex claimed that her husband had punched her, unprovoked, in the face, leaving her disfigured for a fortnight.

I knew that there had been one brief, undeveloped report of physical abuse from Alex years ago, but as a journalist – often more mistrustful of our own medium than anyone else – this could have little or no significance. Alex had since maintained in interviews that whatever had happened that night had been accidental. Couples had fights; she and George had more than most, but, she insisted, she 'gave as good as she got'. There was a streak of perversity in George and I couldn't help wondering if his wife shared it. Intrigued, I had done some background research and discovered that a previous relationship with a footballer had been turbulent too. It was easy to imagine that a woman I didn't know might get off on the physicality of those wrangles, but when I tried to picture George hitting a woman, either now or five years ago, I couldn't do it.

'Want to know what really fucking hurts?' George said finally, having reread the piece. 'That my own wife would lay all this out there for some journalist, some bloodsucker who's just dying to think the worst of me? Sorry,' he shook his head, 'I forget sometimes. I mean, that you . . .'

'Oh, for God's sake, George. If someone like Alex came to me with what she's said here, I'd be delighted. And by the way: what is it you do in your column every week?'

'I give a version of the truth – my version,' he protested. 'She's so young, though,' he sighed with sudden affection, getting up and pacing about the room. 'She doesn't under-stand what these buggers are trying to get out of her most of the time. And she likes the attention. I can understand that – I did too, for a very long time.'

'Oh, I think you still do, George,' I smiled. 'But listen,' I tried to find a diplomatic way of asking the question, 'I don't know Alex but these fights – how serious were they?'

'They were proper fights,' he nodded hesitantly. 'And we've both ended up hurting each other: she's punched me and thrown shoes at me; she's even drawn blood. But I've never hit her – never,' he claimed.

There was something so convincing about those singsong Northern Irish vowels, so heartfelt in George's attempts to sell his side of the story, that despite my better judgement, I always believed him. Perhaps it was his ability to do that which explained the continuing loyalty of the women in his life, despite everything.

'So, do you think that really is it with you two, then? I mean, after what she's said?'

'It?' He looked at me, his bottom lip hanging loose. 'No way.' And what he said next astonished me. 'This is just the start of it: I love my wife and I'm going to get her back.'

Sitting up in bed that afternoon, George was mid-joke, having his blood pressure taken.

'Morning, Trouble, come in. Doc – this is my sitter or guardian angel, depending on what mood she's in. She follows me everywhere.' He arched an eyebrow. 'And I mean *everywhere*.'

'How's the patient?' I sat at the foot of the bed, attempting to halt the movement of George's foot as it travelled towards me beneath the covers.

'The patient,' the doctor said seriously, 'needs to stop treating his body like an amusement arcade. Still,' he ticked a box on his clipboard, 'I'm guessing nobody can tell George Best what to do, can they? But I'm asking you to make an effort while you're here, George. Stephen's said you can stay as long as you like, and I recommend you don't make it less than two weeks this time.'

I baulked: two weeks – was it possible that I could be here two weeks? The place was not as I imagined it – it was more of a spa than a rehab facility (which explained why George didn't have to be brought there under duress) – but wandering about those enervatingly peaceful grounds in the regulation white towelling gown for longer than a few days was hard to contemplate.

'I want you cold turkey, George. Not one sip of alcohol is to pass your lips while you're here. And you'll be reporting to me every day so that I can check your blood pressure and that you've taken these.' He rattled a large, aggressively labelled tub of pills and set them back down on the bedside table. 'Now I know that they make you feel queasy . . .'

George was reacting badly to the babyfied tone and had fixed his eyes on an indefinite point above the door.

'But that is what they are meant to do. Studies have shown—'

'All right, Doc,' George grimaced, warning that his patience was at an end. 'I got you. Now I'd better take this young lady off for her tea. Look at the state of her: I seem to end up making all the women in my life sick with worry.'

I'll never forget the reaction when George first walked into that restaurant. He had stayed at Forest Mere before, over a dozen times, but most people were only ever likely to make a single visit. The mothers and daughters and hen parties giggled in disbelief as George sat down, while the men nudged one another conspicuously. The white robes designed, I assumed, to render guests anonymous, had the opposite effect. When all that identified a person was the face emanating from a shapeless, colourless tarpaulin, features, accents and mannerisms took on a new distinction.

There was the occasional sick or troubled soul identifiable - those who, like George, had shunned real rehab for this vanilla, permissive, health farm. Just a few days into our stay I had caught him staring with ill-concealed disgust at a man I presumed was an alcoholic in the canteen as he tried, with a shaking hand, to bring a spoonful of carrot soup to his mouth. When he got up to leave, orange droppings besmirching the front of his robe, George had followed him loathingly with his eyes, believing, no doubt, that the two of them were worlds apart. It occurred to me then that addicts often confuse extreme behaviour with exceptional behaviour, believing themselves to be unique, superior really, in their torment.

'Quite an entrance, Mr Best,' said the woman to our right as we perused the menus. Bulky beneath her gown, with eyebrows that bore down low across her eyes, giving her a dense look, she seemed to be alone – and lonely. 'Poor you,' she added. 'Can't be easy being in a place like this – being you, I mean.'

In terms of obvious appeal, this woman had nothing to offer George, but like an archaeologist who finds fascination in all stones, not just the precious gems, her sex gave her value. He chatted amiably to her – Tina was her name, a management consultant there 'to recharge her batteries, just like him' – listening patiently to her story.

'Nobody knows I'm here,' she shuddered, having trotted out a précis of the past few years of her life, her inability to have children, the divorce and increasing dependence on food and drink.

'A week away from it all will do you good,' George assured her. 'It's perfect if you just need a peaceful place to find your feet again. That said,' he cast his eye around the room queasily, 'for someone like me, it takes less than five minutes for one of these people to make the call – that's if the press don't already know I've checked in, of course. How long have you been here?'

'A couple of days,' Tina flushed under the thin layer

of clay-coloured foundation she wore. 'I plan on staying another five. Maybe it won't be so boring now that you guys are here.'

When Tina joined us outside afterwards for a walk, I searched George's face for signs of annoyance and was surprised to find that there were none. He was a different man from the previous night: placid, resigned and more than a little comic in his white dressing gown and the trainers he'd insisted on wearing.

After the suffocation of the Surrey barn, I relished the enforced calm at Forest Mere, where I would no longer be solely responsible for George. It took a morning there for me to recognise the atmosphere as that not unpleasant childhood state of paying penance – only in this case it cost you £300 a night. Throwing open my windows as far as they would go, I watched drones in white towelling gowns shuffling about the grounds, appearing like heavenly inmates from behind the shuddering birch trees, and converging now and again with tranquil smiles that hid the madness beneath. Even for the majority who weren't sick, the women who simply considered themselves in need of 'pamper breaks' as the brochure called them, there was something healing about those antiseptic corridors, undertones of bleach not quite drowned out by the citrus-scented candles burning at either end. From behind closed doors buzzed the uninflected murmur of yoga instructors, counsellors and beauticians, the occasional shrill squeak of a trainer in the hallway the only noise to break the therapeutic silence.

Mealtimes, for George, were now all about pill taking, sometimes ten at a time from the same intricately compartmentalised blue box marked with the days of the week. He would throw them down his gullet like the sweets he couldn't live without; make a game out of it, which Tina, who joined us occasionally for lunch and dinner, found endlessly entertaining. Despite these dents to his dignity, the tedium and the medical probes that left him fractious and introspective, Forest Mere had begun to have a positive effect on George.

He and his ghostwriter had penned what he'd laughingly – and in a convincing rendition of my middle-class London accent – referred to as a 'splendidly upbeat' column detailing his decision ('It had to be mine, really, in the end') to clean himself up at Forest Mere, and the office had got their headline.

It was the perfect environment for both our purposes: a place with tight security where other members of the press weren't easily able to gain access, a place where the rules weren't so stringent that George wouldn't be able to relax, and an atmosphere which genuinely appeared to be beneficial. He was enjoying what he called the 'fight-back'. During his two-hour daily gym sessions, he'd try to beat the previous day's record on the running machine and lift ever heavier weights. He wanted, he said, to work his way back to the sporting physique he had once possessed, but which had never come naturally to him.

This violent desire for self-improvement manifested itself in George's every movement. Our walks had become so brisk that I struggled to keep up. Leisurely strolls from the swimming pool to the gym, television room or canteen were businesslike, purposeful affairs and George had developed such a mania of scratching his head with jagged nails, leaving the white paths of his scalp dotted with scabs, that I eventually convinced him to have a manicure at the beauty salon.

'Ever tell anyone about this and you're dead,' he cautioned as I sat beside him, forcing myself to keep a straight face.

'What do you mean?' I replied. 'I think you should put it in your column. Imagine what Roy Keane or Bobbie Charlton will say when they hear about it ...'

Tina, later, had been reduced to such violent spurts of laughter when George had recounted the story that she'd had to beg him to stop talking. There was something odd about her, but I liked the way she treated George: like an amusing companion, not a celebrity. And she seemed to glean as much pleasure from his improvement as I did.

Had Phil been there, he might have warned me not to believe in miracles, but as it was I was caught up in George's enthusiasm – privileged even, to be allowed to witness this about turn. Perhaps the threat of divorce and the idea of losing Alex for good really was enough to make a difference where nothing else had been able. Perhaps, I thought ingenuously, this really would all end happily.

'It's been a while since you've talked about coming home,' my father had commented during a rare phone call I'd been able to make while George was at the gym. 'You will remember, won't you, that none of this is real – that this isn't normal life, I mean?'

'I know that,' I replied, his tone chafing a little. 'But it's all working out well here. They're pleased at the office.'

'Well, I'm sure you're doing well, then.' I heard a summons in the background. 'I mean, you get on with George now, don't you? I hear you talk about him and it's like . . .' There was a pause and I heard his name being called out a second time. 'Listen, I've got to go but take good care, won't you?'

I thought about what my father had said long after he hung up, wondering why there had been a rebuke implicit. Of course I liked George. Just as Phil had said, it would be hard for anyone, given the time I had spent with him, not to. But could we really call ourselves friends when neither one of us was with the other voluntarily? Probably not. And yet thinking of us as two people simply making the best of things depressed me, removing, as it did, the little that was redeeming in our situation. I thought about the way, because he was too lazy to tie them, he tucked his laces into his trainers and the absurd performance he would make, clasping a hand to his heart, whenever I let my hair down from its ponytail ('There is a woman under there – I knew it!') and felt sad, without knowing why.

When Phil arrived a few days later he'd lost weight; from the crumpled shirt he wore, I suspected he'd had a few sleepless nights with the new baby. Still, the pleasure had spread like a flush across his face as I detailed George's progress.

That day, as we walked through the gardens, we did all feel like friends.

'Check out George's walk.'

We were sitting in a gazebo, Phil breaking short our conversation to point out his friend, a white stick man striding back and forth across the lawn, head down, hands manacled behind his back.

'All that mad pacing. Take the football away from his feet and he'll spend the rest of his life looking for it. He's like one of those war veterans, the ones who lose limbs in combat but still feel them.'

'Phantom limbs. I'm just hoping this,' I gestured at George, the grounds, the atmosphere of anaesthetised peace in the air, 'might be giving you some respite too – allow you to enjoy the first few weeks of fatherhood.'

'It has,' he agreed, still reticent. 'I won't lie to you: not having to drop everything to rescue George from a fight or smuggle him out of the back entrance of a pub is a mercy.'

'Do you know that he's now working out twice a day? I think he's convinced that if he gets back on track Alex might give him another chance.'

Silently, we both considered how unlikely that seemed.

'How does he appear to you?'

Shielding our eyes from the sun, we turned in unison to look at him.

'I think he's enjoying the "comeback", as he puts it,' he said finally. 'George used to quite like getting a bit out of shape on holiday, or during a drinking binge, just for the pleasure of having something to work at again. He's always loved training, and being fit, which sounds funny when you think of what he's done to his body over the years. Old-fashioned Protestant guilt, maybe ...' He smiled but his eyes kept their tarnished quality.

Eastern mood music drifted down from an open window above – one of the massage rooms, perhaps – laughably ill-suited to the Englishness of the surroundings, the croquet and the rich click of tennis balls in the distance.

'God, I'd go mad if I had to stay here longer than a day or two,' murmured Phil. 'I don't know how you stand it.'

In the mid-distance, George had come up behind a neat rectangle of women performing aerobics, and was making indecent gestures for our benefit.

Phil groaned; I laughed.

'I'm amazed he hasn't been chucked out of here yet.'

I waited a moment.

'Have you spoken to Alex at all?'

'Yes, several times. She's still insisting she doesn't want to talk to him, but I think that despite everything, there might still be a chance for them, I really do.'

'Do you think she's still in love with him?'

Phil looked at me curiously. 'I can't say I've ever thought about it.'

It was my turn to be curious. 'What? You've never wondered what's kept her with him all these years?'

'I have no doubt that she cares about him, loves him,' he made a vague gesture through the air with his cigarette, as though it were all semantics, 'or whatever. But don't forget how young she was when she married him. I'd say there's a fair amount of bitterness there and a fair amount of anxiousness on her part that she gets back what she put in. Watch the two of them together and there's a bond there made up of all sorts of things. And yes, I'm sure there's love there too. One thing's for sure – divorce wasn't what Alex got into this for. She's not like some of these women now: calculating their settlements as they walk down the aisle. But George,' he swallowed, 'well, if he loses her then things really could get messy. She's the only thing that keeps him sane.'

'He's been calling her. Most days, I think. Says she won't pick up.'

'She told me.'

'The paper has this crazy idea of reuniting them here – doing a big piece on them giving it another try with pictures of the happy couple and everything.'

I left the idea hanging there.

'Oh really?' Phil raised an ironic eyebrow. 'Does it matter to you lot if they want to give it another try?'

I shrugged. 'Why get bogged down in the detail?'

'She will come around . . .' He ran a thumb and forefinger down the line of his jaw. 'I've been begging her to come and see him here. I've told her he's off the booze, trying hard to stay that way and that it's all for her benefit. But don't forget that she's seen all this before – many, many times. And if I know George and he doesn't start getting somewhere soon, he won't be sticking to this new leaf for long.'

'But look at him.'

Our eyes sought him out and found him at the corner of the vegetable garden. Sulking a little that we had turned our attention away, he was talking to Tina, who, as was her wont, had appeared from nowhere.

Sheltered from the afternoon sunlight, drenched in russet shadows, his face and limbs seemed like those of a much younger man – certainly still those of an athlete. Screwing up my eyes, I tried to picture him as the winged-footed young man I had seen on that TV screen, playing with his own genius like a piano player dashing off a light trill of notes. Then he stepped forward into the sunlight and that mouth, a mouth that used to blow kisses at beauty queens and bellow out victory chants, a mouth once blown up to fifty times its real size to advertise aftershave on a billboard in Oxford Circus, was reduced to a mass of jowl.

'I'll give Alex another try, OK? That's all I can do. And you just do your best to keep him on the straight and narrow in the meantime.'

'I'm not sure I'm able to make George do anything he doesn't want to do,' I smiled, standing up.

'Oh I wouldn't do yourself down.' Phil snorted as a memory bubbled up. 'You know what he said the other night? The night we got here? You were walking off towards your room while we waited for the doctor, and he watched you until you disappeared, then turned to me and said: "That, Phil, is a real lady." Course he then turned his attentions to the receptionist, but I thought it was, I dunno, nice.'

There was no room for niceness that afternoon: George had decided to give me a football lesson. In a pair of his shorts, a T-shirt bought from the gift shop which preached, in curly writing, 'Learn to love life again', and trainers borrowed from another guest we charged across the lawn, George dancing about, the ball invisibly attached to his feet, before the assembled crowd. Great cheers went up when he scored, and as I watched him play up to their adulation, I wondered whether in a perverse way, addiction had made him capable of a new, clean, joy. Having revelled in the sinister world of self-abuse, there must surely be some relief in finding your natural reactions uncorrupted at the end of it.

I liked it when George was infantile and playful. He played ping pong in the games room with the enthusiasm of a young boy, later lying mummified by his robe at the side of the pool, where he would gorge on some new thriller from the boutique. I wonder now whether George had a capacity to enjoy life that surpassed other peoples'. Psychiatrists like to put excess and addiction down to the deficiencies in a person's life, but isn't it sometimes just a form of gluttony? Occasionally, when I had observed George in the act of drinking, I had wondered whether his alcoholism were a literal translation of a desire to press his mouth greedily to the font.

'Drugs never appealed to me,' he volunteered that night. 'Funny really, considering what I'm like. I once went to see a shrink who diagnosed me with having an "excessive personality disorder". Biggest waste of £500 ever; I could have told him that.'

We were sitting in George's bedroom playing poker for matchsticks and he was in the expansive, complaisant mood that often preceded a slight depression in him.

'When I was young, I wanted to do it all – and I could. I felt like I was on top of the world. People called me a god and, arrogant as it sounds, I felt like I was a god. Sort of untouchable. So I would go on a three-day binge, just disappear, and nobody knew where I was. I didn't even know where I'd been, most of the time.'

We both laughed, easily, companionably, eyes still on the cards.

'But there were things I didn't do, either because they didn't interest me or because they didn't seem right. I would never have dreamed of drinking before a big game. A lot of them would have a slug of scotch in the dressing rooms but I would just munch on chocolate to get my energy up. And I really didn't understand cigarettes or joints ... quite a few of the lads would smoke those in my day. But people talk a whole load of codswallop about the sixties; anyone would think that we were all wandering the streets high on acid for a decade the way they go on about it now. Fact is there's more of that and worse nowadays, with footballers taking the lot. I don't get it. Do you reckon,' lowering his eyelashes over those dimmed irises, he grinned impishly up at me from his propped position, 'do you reckon that I'd be in better shape now if I'd gone down that route?'

'Well, it's never too late to start, George. See you and raise you ten.'

'That's true. That would make a good one for my column, wouldn't it? "Alcohol's not working for me so I've moved on to ecstasy ..."' He paused. 'We were so young, though, you know? When we first left our families ... no wonder some of us went off the rails. And there was nobody there to look out for us, nobody there to prepare us for the attention like there is now.'

I didn't like it when George got into blame – it was to his credit that he rarely did.

'You look at these young lads, and they're all cosseted and "managed" to within an inch of their lives.'

'Maybe that's one of your legacies ...'

'Great. Glad to hear that my messing up has been useful.'

'And anyway, some people are probably naturally better equipped to deal with the whole celebrity thing than others.'

'Yeah? Maybe you're right. It has to do with the age you become famous, no doubt, and your background – but also whether you can handle it. I couldn't.'

There was a question I had always wanted to ask; now seemed as good a time as any.

'Do you think you would still have become an alcoholic without those pressures?'

'Of that lifestyle?' He pretended to think about it, but I could tell that he had long ago decided on the answer. 'I think fame sort of turns the dial up, you know? Exaggerates and accentuates everything. And there aren't the barriers of money or decency like there are with most people. If you like women, you can have as many as you want; if you like booze, there will always be someone willing to buy you of a bottle of champagne. It's about there being too much choice, really. Life as an all-you-can-eat buffet. My mum ...' He paused. He had only rarely mentioned her before, but never her alcoholism. 'Well, I sometimes think it was there all the time, dormant or something.' He broke into a sudden smile. 'At first she couldn't believe it all: she'd line up the different shampoo bottles I'd bring back from hotels in Spain, Italy, America in the bathroom. They'd just sit there on the windowsill gathering dust, like ornaments or something, and I'd say, "Mum, I brought them back for you to wash your hair with – that's what they're there for," but she thought they were too fancy to use.'

He paused, and I sensed him slipping further into the tenebrous recesses of his own mind.

'So stupid ... so stupid ...' He'd forgotten about his cards, abandoned in his open palm for me to see. 'Some of the lads did love it,' he murmured.

'Love what?'

He looked up, as though surprised to see me still there.

'Travelling, but – and this'll sound stupid to you, or spoilt – I never could get used to those hotel beds, even the five-star ones. They never felt as comfortable to me as the one back home. It didn't matter if they were made up with the best sheets, and God, there were silk pillowcases in this one place in LA … I swear they were the softest thing I'd ever touched – but they always felt funny to me.'

He had explained, back in Surrey, how drink had helped to dull the crippling homesickness he had never grown out of. And on the surface, of course, everyone was living it up: back at the hotel bar after games, in the airport lounges waiting for flights, during flights and celebrating once back on home soil, there was always a reason to drink. It took him years, long after his career had peaked, to realise and then admit his problem: that he didn't drink like them.

'I knew that I was a big drinker, but we all were, and who really knows how much other people are drinking? I wasn't there counting their pints. Plus, I was smaller than a lot of the other lads, so I would use that as an excuse if I had a funny turn, or a hangover. Now, I wonder whether being as fit as I was actually counted against me: I couldn't see or feel what the drink was doing to me. More than that, I couldn't believe that it would do anything to me.'

His physique had also been a factor, I suspected. Reclining on the bed as he was now, head tilted back against the headboard, features sleekened by gravity, George appeared twenty years younger, recalling the deliberately blasé poses of magazine adverts I'd never seen, but could imagine. Good looks shield people from reality: behaviour, good and bad rebounding cleanly off them. For George it was another reason to ignore the warnings: how could anything that beautiful be rotting inside? Even now, despite his self-abuse, the crumbs of that film star allure were still there, and he still knew how to use them.

'I wish I'd known you then.' I said it without thinking.

He blinked, touched but uncomfortable at the remark.

'When?'

'Before all this,' I shrugged, adding to myself, *When you were the person I keep hearing about, the one that you are now only a fraction of the time.*

He started to nod, but thought better of it.

'The problem is, that when I'm so pissed that I've lost it, that I'm swearing in front of you and . . .' shame forced his eyes away from mine, '. . . threatening you, like I did at the barn, I feel as much like myself as I do sitting here now.'

A whoop of female voices – one of the hen parties staying at the hotel – rose from the garden, but George didn't smile.

'I'm sorry about that, by the way.'

He said it so softly that I wasn't sure I had heard him, but the accompanying look was fervent enough to explain the enduring loyalty of the women in his life.

'And the thing is,' he was anxious to move on from the apology, 'I'm not sure there ever has been a less complicated time. Not since I left home. And I'm probably nicer now than I was back in the day.'

'Jesus.'

'I know. Go on then,' he put his cards down with a flourish. 'Show me what you've got.'

His palm – clammy and smooth, but honest, somehow – lay upturned and empty on the bed. He gestured for my hand, curling his fingers over mine, and I noticed that a square indentation along one of his cuticles - an old war wound from the pitch perhaps – marred their symmetry.

'I'm going to ask you something I think I already know the answer to – and you can be honest, OK?'

'OK.' With no idea what he was going to say, I was apprehensive.

'Do you have a crush on me? And don't lie, because you're . . .'

'No,' I laughed.

'. . . embarrassed, because you're not the first and you sure as hell won't be the last . . .'

'No, George.' I wasn't sure he was joking. 'I swear on your new sobriety that I don't have a crush on you.'

'OK.' He looked back at his cards with a humouring smile. 'But that's not much to go on, is it? And remember that when you spend a lot of time with a person it's easy to—'

'George!'

'All right, all right. Don't get your knickers in a twist. I realise that you hated me when we first met, you made that pretty clear.'

'I never hated you – I just didn't care about you. Thought you were an old pisshead, which you are.'

'Was, Trouble, was. But just you watch: I'll come good.'

As I showered before dinner that night, following a conversation with the news desk about what was now being referred to in grandiose terms as 'the reunion', I found myself querying whether it was a good idea to jeopardise George's newfound balance for a meeting so fraught with emotional turmoil. As it was, the decision was already out of our hands.

When George didn't join me for breakfast the following morning, as he had done every day of our stay, it was clear that something was up.

'I just saw him down the gym,' said Tina, pleased to be providing me with the information. 'And I have to tell you, for an alcoholic who had a liver transplant a year ago, the guy is in pretty good shape.'

I watched as she scraped the last of her scrambled eggs off her plate, pressing down hard with her fork so as to catch every last, creamy slur.

'What about you, Tina?' I wasn't sure how to phrase it without sounding patronising. 'Is it doing you good, being here?'

'Oh yes,' she nodded, the tight knot of her hair bobbing its own assent. 'I wish I could stay longer now.'

A smile rippled across her face, fleeting as a breeze across water, and her eyes narrowed.

'And George?'

I nodded. 'He's doing well, very well. I'm hoping he's turned a corner, but I know so little about alcoholism that it's hard to say for sure.'

'Has Alex been in to see him yet?'

I kept it vague. 'I guess she'll come by when she thinks he's ready.'

'So, it's not all over between them? Or was this,' she jangled her braceleted hand around at the canteen, 'part of the deal with her? That George should stay here a certain amount of time . . .'

Unable to answer her questions, and concerned by George's absence, I excused myself.

'Sorry – tell me to buzz off when I'm being a nosy cow,' her hand was on my sleeve.

'Don't be silly. You're worried about him; we all are.'

There was no need: George's good humour persevered as he worked towards what he saw as an inevitable reunion with Alex. His efforts at the gym redoubled, and lunch and tea times were spent engaged in animated discussions about the future – moving to Spain perhaps, but certainly away from the barn in Surrey, tainted now by bad memories. Still, the lull of those first days at Forest Mere had given way to twitchiness. He would disappear at frequent intervals, wherever we were, and (because, he said, of the diuretic effect of his new pills) seemed unable to sit still. I suspected that he was in greater physical discomfort than he was letting on, yet there was progress: his face had come alive again.

'So, do you want the good news or the good news?'

Slowing from a 10.5 kilometre run to a brisk walk, George's voice came out in rhythmic bursts over the purr of the machine, as though someone were intermittently pressing down hard on his diaphragm.

I settled myself in front of him, with my back to the wall. 'Go on.'

'I just ran two kilometres at an incline of three. Not bad, eh? And,' with that elastic Irish accent, he dragged the conjunction out, 'Alex has agreed to come here tomorrow to talk. Isn't that great?'

He treated me to a vaudeville smile.

'She's said she might even think about that big interview you wanted, a photo shoot, the lot. How do I look?'

'A mess.'

This wasn't quite true: great flowers of sweat discoloured the Manchester United shirt he wore beneath the arms and in a wide V down the chest, but there were explosions of pink in both cheeks, normally studies in shades of grey, and the pupils appeared less murky than they had been of late.

I should have been pleased. After all, I could offer this up as my victory to the office, but the forced, public nature of this 'reunion' made me question both George and Alex's motivations.

As he stepped off the running machine, mopping his brow with one end of the hand towel tied around his neck, George panted, 'Come on. Let's have a jacuzzi first to celebrate.'

I called the office from a cubicle in the changing room.

'If this comes off, and you really do manage to get them in the same room, we need them on the record talking about the fights, how they're going to move past them and give their marriage another try. You know the stuff.'

'See him?'

We were alone in the jacuzzi, up to our necks in bubbles that tickled our chins when we spoke. Pulling a hand laced with foam from the depths, he pointed to a black and white still of Warren Beatty hanging on the wall.

'I had his fiancée once.' He sank down deeper, careful to keep his nose and mouth just above the water, two sharp points on an island of pink skin. 'We swapped a few women, me and Warren – he went out with my ex-wife Angie, too.'

I made a face. 'George ...'

'I do apologise,' he caught a mouthful of froth and used it to turn his voice into a Disney gurgle. 'Didn't realise you were such a prude. But, my God, that girl was a beauty. Didn't mention she had a boyfriend until we were lying in bed afterwards. "I'm engaged," she said. "OK," I said. "And how seriously do you take it?"'

We both laughed.

'To be honest,' he shifted and the water swirled

comfortably around us like a blanket. 'It made her a much more attractive catch. I don't like it when women are too easy to get.'

With one grey curl stuck damply to his forehead he looked ridiculous, like an aged cherub.

'I'd called her up and invited her out for dinner and it turned into a four-day bed-in. He,' we both looked back over at the portrait, and those racks and racks of American teeth, 'was out in LA filming, so we thought we were safe, but on day three the press found out, and it sort of added to the excitement of things.' He smiled, blowing away a bubble from the corner of his mouth. 'She and Beatty didn't stay together anyway.'

That night, Phil came to visit. Deflated by his lack of expression when I'd described, a little too rapturously, George's continued transformation as we walked down from reception to the dining room, I consoled myself by thinking that he, like Alex, had probably had his senses numbed by years of ups and downs with George.

'It all sounds good,' he nodded noncommittally. 'But don't ...' He seemed to rethink whatever he was going to say. 'Never mind. Where is this man anyway? And what's he done with Beastie?'

'It was not a dump,' chuckled George, laying down his knife and fork.

'Maybe not,' Phil conceded, 'but trust me, Celia, it wasn't the classiest place. This joint was in the middle of nowhere, somewhere en route to Heathrow, with a chintzy little conservatory. You and Alex were originally going to get married either at Chelsea Football Ground or the Belvedere in Holland Park – remember?'

'Yeah. But the paps didn't get us, did they?'

'I don't think even they would have ventured that far afield, George.'

The two men fell about.

'All right, you've made your point. But I was lucky Alex still wanted to go through with it, what with me calling off the wedding the first time ...'

'... because you "fell in love".'

'Hey,' George got up, still laughing. 'I thought I was in love. Oh and Hughsie, look at my eyes: they're almost back. Excuse me. I'll just be a second.'

Phil followed him warily with his eyes as he left the room. 'Where's he going?' He gestured towards George's half-eaten Thai curry. 'He's barely touched his food.'

'It's the pills,' I explained. 'I think they ... well, I'm not sure I really want to know what they do.'

Phil nodded slowly.

'So, you've been taking your pills, George?' he said, with a deliberate note I couldn't quite place, as soon as his friend had sat down again.

George didn't look up. 'Yes.'

'Have you?'

'I've just said I have.' He threw me an incredulous look. 'Do you know what the worst thing is about being me, Trouble?'

His smile had frozen.

'That look – right there.' He pointed to Phil.

'I didn't say a word,' Phil said evenly, without looking up from his plate of pasta.

160

'I know you didn't.'

After this odd exchange, the conversation came close to resuming its previous tone, but something had been lost. Soon after, with a yawn and a stretch, George urged Phil to 'Drive home carefully' and disappeared upstairs.

'You two and your spats,' I sighed, reaching for a tooth-pick. 'You're like a husband and wife, second-guessing each other the whole time. Still, you must be pleased with him, no? He's a different man to . . . What?'

Laying his knife and fork down on his plate, Phil looked over at me. 'You know why he's on such good form, don't you?' He dabbed at corners of his mouth with a napkin. 'Because he's drunk.'

I slept badly that night, unable to find a comfortable position. Eventually the ominous gulps of the radiators contrived to send me into a tight, angry sleep. When I awoke, my hands were rolled into fists, my chest damp with sweat, and instinc-tively, I knew that things were about to get a whole lot worse.

George wasn't in his bedroom, the breakfast room or the gym, and I scoured the grounds, rueing the white robe that made it difficult for me to walk briskly, let alone run. Across the lawn, disappearing into the orchard and ambling down the towpath beside the lake, anonymous white figures started their day, alone or in Mormon-like cliques. A grey-haired man with his back to me on a bench by the pool turned out not to be George, but a woman with mournful eyes and a welcoming smile.

'You haven't seen . . . You haven't seen George, have you?' *George*. Banal and familiar – yet the Christian name was enough.

'No,' the woman turned her body eagerly towards me. 'You've lost him? Sit down for a moment ...'

But I was already walking back fast towards the house, remembering the shaded enclave outside the games room where George liked to sit, on a green garden chair buffered by years of winter winds.

'George?'

He didn't look up from his magazine, the first I had seen him read since we'd got there.

'George.'

When he did raise his eyes they were so furious that I wondered what I had done wrong.

'Alex rang,' he crossed his arms. 'She won't be coming today.'

He was crushed.

'Maybe tom—'

'Not tomorrow either.'

'Why not?'

'Because of this.'

He handed me the magazine, crumpling up the cover with his hands as he did so, like a piece of rubbish.

I took in the headline: 'Best's Drunken Nights at Health Farm'. I read the piece very quickly, still standing, with the conviction that it was mostly lies. According to the article, George had started drinking again a day or two after arriving at Forest Mere, and had been engaged in a constant binge since then. A star-struck local boy had been flattered to be asked to carry out the booze commissions, smuggling in wine and then vodka, because it was easier to carry around in small quantities. The details were absurd: according to the piece, George had kept a Lucozade bottle in the pocket of his robe filled with booze and would even work out drunk, sipping white wine from it as he ran on the treadmill. But it was what he had allegedly been telling people about Alex which was the worst. Variations on comments made to me in Malta, when he had confessed to worrying that 'fame really matters to her', peppered the piece.

One look at his face told me that the journalist had got almost every detail right. Yet I was surprised to find that my anger at George, for drinking again, for lying to me, Phil and Alex, was almost completely surpassed by the betrayal. For some reason, I was on his side. There was only one person who could have sold this story, and that was Tina.

'So that night, the night we sat by the lake – you took Tina back to your room and got pissed together?'

He nodded.

'Wasn't it obvious that she was going to go to the press, George?'

'You tell me.' He shifted so that his whole body, pathetically insubstantial in its robe, faced me. 'You deal with those people all the time. Aren't people like her exactly the kind you're meant to be keeping me away from? Just look at her: she's a screw-up who saw a chance to make a quick few grand – or maybe that was all she was after from the beginning. Not that we'll ever know either way.'

His words crashed into one another, their natural cadence lost, and I realised without any particular emotion that he was drunk. Instinctively I looked down at the pocket of his gown, making out with bitter amusement the shape of a Lucozade bottle beneath the towelling.

'You know what?' I could hear the shortness of breath, the struggling of his internal organs. 'I reckon my big mistake was getting involved with newspapers – with any of you lot – to begin with.'

He hadn't expected me to laugh at this, but I couldn't help myself: if he wanted me to feel guilty, he'd be disappointed. George was hardly a novice when it came to the press; he'd been using them for his own gain since before I was born. The initial thought I'd had in Malta – that I didn't stand a chance of controlling him – had been right. Everything between then and now that had convinced me otherwise, hadn't meant a thing.

Irked by my lack of reaction, George got up and walked quickly around the corner and into the building, his trainers squeaking a little as he went.

Later, there was one thing I never understood: why hadn't Tina – an opportunist whose decision to sell her story was hardly surprising in retrospect – left Forest Mere before the piece appeared?

By the time I guessed what might happen, it was too late. A phone call from reception was the first I heard of it.

'We don't know what to do.' The meek-mannered brunette who had been so helpful during our stay sounded on the verge of tears, and I could hear George's profanities in the background. 'Could you come down, please?'

George was standing inches away from Tina when I got there. Legs set apart, she stared back at him defiantly. The suitcase behind her indicated that she had, at least, been about to leave when George had tracked her down.

'I don't know how many times I can say this, George:

it wasn't me. Don't you think I'm shocked too? I thought you were making a breakthrough here and there you were drinking the whole time.'

She was convincing – up to a point.

'You can't carry on blaming other people for everything, George,' she went on. 'You were lying to your lovely wife and you deserved to be found out.'

The tension rose a notch. If I knew George, any talk of Alex would rapidly inflame the situation. A gaggle of people had collected now, their faces displaying the polite interest of theatre spectators.

'Don't you dare talk about my wife,' he warned. 'You know nothing about me; nothing about my marriage.'

'Well, I know she must be a saint, George . . .'

It was the intimacy of that Christian name that did it. If it weren't for the car dealer there on a weekend break with his girlfriend lunging forward and deflecting George's hand as it flew towards Tina's face, he would have broken her nose.

After something like that, the air takes on a thicker quality. I watched as people moved about in a daze, rubbing Tina's back and murmuring words of astonishment and reassurance to one another. Meanwhile, George walked straight out of the front door.

I had wondered whether we had been cut off, but no; my boss was still there.

'You think he was going to hit her?'

'Well, he wasn't going to wipe her nose.'

'Right.' A pause. 'This doesn't look good for us, this really doesn't. If this gets out, well, we can't be employing woman-beaters . . . And do you know where he is now?'

'No idea. Nobody seems to.'

'That's not really good enough. I need you to find him, pronto. He won't be far – he doesn't have a car so it shouldn't be difficult. And when you do, stay with him. He's a loose cannon at this point, and if he starts mouthing off to any other newspapers now, we could wind up looking pretty damned stupid.'

On my way back to my room, I noticed that George's door was ajar.

'George?'

But there was no one. Just the paraphernalia left behind by a hasty exit, the debris of a double life. A crumpled Benson and Hedges packet – Tina's brand – in the bin now made sense. One thing bothered me: how could I have spent so much time in George's company without smelling the alcohol on his breath? The answer was in the cupboard beneath the sink in the bathroom: bottles of mouthwash and Extra-Strong Mints – everything you might need to disguise that bite of wine. The level of deception, the realisation that I was the enemy, hit me. As I sat down on the bed my ankle knocked against something cold. I knelt down and lifted the bedspread, activating, as I did so, an unexpected tang of urine. He hadn't known how to dispose of the empty Chardonnay bottles, and there were dozens of them. Wedged beneath one was an empty family-sized pack of wine gums.

The nearest pub in Liphook was a twenty-minute walk away, but he wasn't there. Nor was there any sign of him at The Links Tavern, The Royal Anchor or The Railway Inn.

Back at Forest Mere, I went straight to Stephen Purdew's office.

'I know, I know: he's taken off.' In previous conversations

we'd had concerning his friend of twenty years, Stephen's tone had always been cavalier. Now he sounded scared. 'He came to see me and I couldn't get any sense out of him. He said he wanted to get away for a bit – from you, from everyone.'

'It's because of that woman.' I looked down at my hands, which were trembling, and then back at Stephen. 'Tina: we think she sold a story to the press. Now he assumes that other people will be—'

'I don't know,' he cut in. 'He was quoting from that book he's always on about, *The Dice Man*: something about getting on a plane and drinking on a beach. Something about disappearing. I've never heard him talk that way before. I got this feeling that it was his way . . .' he took a deep breath. 'I think he was threatening to end it all . . .' Grabbing his jacket from the back of the chair, he managed a worried smile in my direction. 'Want my advice? Go back to London and get back to work. You're in over your head here.'

CHAPTER SIX

PROJECT 'Y' WAS LARGELY agreed to be the least rewarding job on the paper. A sequence of journalists had worked on it over the past year and got nowhere; I had been working on it for ten days now, trying to inject new blood into a story that was destined never to be published. It was my penance for letting George get away, that much had been made clear, but there was something therapeutic about the daily plod that had become my life over the past fortnight. I had made no progress. Nobody either knew or cared, but the long moments of tedium the job afforded me suited my current state.

With George still uncontactable, his column was temporarily being filled by another celebrity. To think how much people would read into that footnote, *George Best is away*, now.

I felt removed from everyone and suffocated by the interest in George, both at work and outside it. Finding myself unable – or unwilling – to describe George as he really was, I told people what they wanted to hear, customising statements to provide maximum satisfaction.

'He was a total maniac,' I'd tell the expectant semicircle of friends at the pub. 'Total maniac.'

'Drunk 24/7 – really?' they would ask.

'Oh yeah. Just sat there downing whole bottles of vodka.'

The accepted prognosis proved correct, they tended to move on.

There had been a missed call from him late one Thursday, but when I rang back, the phone had rung out. I pictured him staring at my number on the screen with a drink in his hand, having changed his mind, and wondered at how toxic damaged people were – somehow able to affect even those on the very periphery of their worlds.

Just one person, a female reporter in her late fifties, was able to recognise my state.

'People get like this after jobs sometimes,' she said, standing beside me at the washbasins in the ladies and quietly observing me in the mirror. 'It makes sense really. You're thrown into something, something either weird or gruesome a lot of the time, and then you're just expected to pick up the pieces of your old life where you left off. It can't have been easy being with that disgusting old drunk.'

Had my opinion of George been as straightforward as that, I might have found the transition back to normality a little easier, but the reality was that George wasn't an easy character to forget.

There had been snippets in the papers – a sighting at Gatwick and another at a resort in southern Spain – but those were both a week ago; since then there had been nothing.

Phil had rung me once, sweetly, to apologise, although I should have been the one apologising for my own gullibility.

He assured me that he hadn't heard from George either, and seemed worried that the TV contracts and endorsements he had fought hard to maintain would start to collapse one by one. Soon, he said, the column would be George's only earner. I didn't have the heart to say what we both knew: that the column too would be taken away unless he could be found soon in some sort of stable condition.

'I hope you don't see any of it as being your fault,' Phil had insisted. 'I tried to warn you.'

I had expected George to call me, but when he hadn't, even from a beach bar after two jugs of sangria, it made me think that he had either put me in a loathed box marked 'journalist', or that he had never felt any particular fondness towards me in the first place. I suppose I had imagined that, alone abroad, he might have felt vulnerable enough, even for a second, to need me.

Only, of course, he wasn't abroad and he wasn't alone.

'He's back.' The paper landed with momentum on my desk, sending pens rolling on to the floor. 'And he's got company. Any idea who she is?'

The picture could have been anybody – unless you knew it was George. Only a third of his face was visible to the camera, engrossed as he was in his female companion. His beard had grown long, quickly, the flash of the camera bleaching those greying temples so that he looked a good decade older than when I'd last seen him, in direct contrast to her. She was in her late twenties or early thirties, I estimated, with aquiline, Mediterranean features, carved expertly to catch the light in just such a way. Eyes, opaque beneath hooded lids, stared brazenly at the camera. But it was the juxtaposition of the white-blonde hair with those Italianate skin tones which made up the arresting whole.

'Well?'

'I have no idea who she is.'

'Right. Well, he's shacked up with her in a council house in Ewell, so I'm guessing they haven't just met. Mind you, this is George Best we're talking about.'

'Exactly. I'll bet they *have* just met. Course, he's got nowhere else to go, has he?' I was thinking out loud. 'Alex is back in the barn; apparently she's kicked him out. And he hates hotels.'

Having skimmed through the text, which told me little more than the picture (nobody knew who the girl was – just that she had been spotted out with George twice in Reigate) and registered that my inability to recognise this girl would only be added to my catalogue of incompetencies, I handed the paper back to my boss.

'Keep that,' he said, walking off, 'you'll need it to find out who she is.'

If only every job were as easy as it had been to unmask Gina. One look at our mystery girl told me that this was a woman known to the local beauticians.

'Oh, you mean Gina!' gushed the owner of the second place I tried, on Ewell High Street, three inches of creped cleavage on display. 'Everybody's talking about her and George. Not that I'm saying there's anything funny going on. But they've become friends, haven't they? Which is nice. Not hard to imagine how she caught his eye, though. She's a beautiful girl, Gina: was in the magazines, catalogues and everything. I remember this one advert she did . . .'

But all I really wanted was Gina's number. Fifty pounds got it for me, scrawled in curly writing on the back of a flyer advertising free eyebrow tints. When I called it, a girl picked up at the first ring – only it wasn't Gina; this girl couldn't have been older than six or seven. A stilted conversation ensued, during which the girl dropped the phone twice. Finally, a woman came on and asked rather aggressively whether I was selling double glazing, because she'd said she couldn't afford any last week and nothing had changed.

'No,' I explained hurriedly, worried she might hang up. 'Is that Gina? You don't know me, but I'm a friend of George's.'

I had thought it all through on the drive down and decided that the only way to be sure that Gina would see me was to invent (it wasn't so much a lie as an elaboration) a potential health scare involving George, some new pills he needed, and a handover.

'I know he wants to be left alone, but the thing is, I've got his pills here, and if he doesn't take them—'

'You're not a reporter, are you?' she interrupted.

'No,' I replied, because it seemed easier. 'I'm a friend of Phil's.'

'Well, you'd better drop them round, then.'

I smiled at a passer-by in the street; that had been easy.

'No, wait.' I could picture George shaking his head and mouthing 'no'. 'I'll pick them up for him, meet me at Café Rouge in Reigate in half an hour.'

She was there before me, and I was early. Nerves, I guessed. George would have known it was me and warned her. Only something – and this intrigued me – had made her come anyway.

When she stood to greet me I knew immediately that it was curiosity, quite simply, that had made her come. They had similar looks, she and Alex, impregnable glamour-girl sheens which belonged in the pages of magazines, but where George's wife had an athletic resilience about her slim figure, this girl was sinuously slender. Blonde, with small, adolescent breasts hoisted high beneath a baby-pink sweatshirt exposing a shadowy curve of belly, she drew looks of nauseous desire from every man there. She was brown; not the kind of brown you get in Britain, abroad, or anywhere, for that matter: perfect, toneless, caramel brown from her armpits down to the arches of her insteps. Her denim skirt was inexpensive, but the thighs and legs spilling out rendered it precious-looking – a thing of value. Although the outfit was provocative in the extreme, her flip-flops – pink with diamanté hearts adorning the clear plastic straps – meant that the overall result was more teenage Lolita than working girl.

'Celia, is it?' She approached cautiously. 'Listen, I shouldn't be here. George is in a right old huff. Says you are a journalist, and that he's told you before to leave him alone.'

'I am, Gina – I should have said on the phone, but I thought you wouldn't come. George and I have been working together for a while.' I paused, not sure which way this was going to go. 'And it's just really important that he gets these.'

I put the packet, provided by Phil, on the table, giving her the option of taking them and leaving, but hoping she wouldn't.

'Would you like a cappuccino or something, Gina?'

173

'All right – they do nice ones here.'

'Two of those, please,' I told the waiter. 'Is he OK, Gina? Is George OK?'

Moving suspicious eyes over me, as though trying to guess what I knew about their relationship, she began to chip away at the silver polish on a thumbnail.

'He seems fine. I think he just wants to be left alone.'

You know nothing about him yet, do you? I thought to myself. *Not a thing.*

'I'm a friend of his, Gina, as well as a journalist. He was doing so well at Forest Mere and . . .'

'I know who you are.' She sucked the froth from her spoon in one clean gesture. 'George told me that you were sent to keep an eye on him. Says the paper wants him to start writing his column again. My brother always used to read it, you know.' Brown elbows at far corners of the little table, fingers locked into a knot in between those pink velour-clad breasts, she leaned forward. 'I think he should get back to it, too. The *News of the World*'s my paper – but everyone said his column was good. Anyway,' she shrugged, 'I think he needs the money; he said he does. That cow . . .' She bit her lip. 'Alex . . . apparently she's going to make things really difficult for him.'

I was surprised by her venom.

'I don't know what's going on in their marriage, Gina, but I agree with you about the column – he does need the money. Besides, I actually think he enjoys talking over what he's going to put in it every week with his ghost-writer. And he owes it to his fans, don't you think?' I added for good measure. 'They don't know what's going on right now and they're worried.'

174

I told her about the phonecalls and letters that we would get about George – the fans suggesting exorcism or equine therapy to help him beat his addiction – omitting to mention that a good portion of them were no longer clamouring for his return but asking why the paper continued to employ a drunk.

'So what do you want me to do?'

She had finished her cappuccino, and our chat had provided me with everything the news desk wanted to know about George's new woman. Now, I would leave it up to Gina to see whether she could talk him around.

'Look, I'm the last person in the world who wants to bother George, but he needs to be careful.

'If his fans turn against him, that wouldn't be good.'

A flash of something, too fleeting to identify, crossed her face and I wondered what it was she was after. Was it as mundane as money and fame? Getting that beautiful face into the papers? Did she have longer-term plans? Or had she really fallen in love with George? There was something childishly unformed about Gina, a single mother whose life, so far, had consisted of a succession of ill-fated relationships. She was right to think, as I suspected she did, that she had always been destined for better things.

'Let me talk to him,' she said when we got outside.

'Can't I give you a lift home?' I pushed, hoping she would rise to the bait.

'Better not,' she flung back, and I watched her slap off down the street in her flip-flops.

'Good job,' my boss said slowly, cocking his head to one side as I recounted the conversation. 'If you really think Gina might convince him to honour his contract, you should try and stay in with her. Although I'd be bloody surprised if she does come through for us.'

But she did, and I wasn't. From the way she had laid out her life for me over a cappuccino, I had known that there was something beautifully straightforward about Gina.

'He'll see you,' she exhaled down the phone the following morning. 'Says you're trouble, but he'll see you.'

The conversation left me smiling. And there was something else: now that I was no longer angry with George, I was looking forward to seeing him again.

The article we'd run revealing Gina's identity hadn't done us any favours. Other tabloid editors had ordered full background checks and, within forty-eight hours, former modelling shots of 'the new woman in George's life' had surfaced, alongside potted histories. Gina's supposed indiscretions were the usual, run-of-the-mill stuff; the jumble of fact and fiction, kneaded and rolled out into an unpalatable paste, likely to make up the lives of most pretty girls. A female 'friend' had insisted that Gina was a party girl, who liked a drink herself. 'I remember watching her get completely legless once in the pub,' said Joyce White, full of the joys of sisterhood. 'By the end of the night she was all over the place.' No article was complete without that irrepressible sniff of personal opinion: 'I can't say I'm surprised that she's ended up with George Best. Those two deserve each other.'

The press, far from sated by these morsels, were clogging up Gina's narrow street. Two cameramen sat on her doorstep, while a third had wedged himself into the plastic slide which took up the three square feet of her neighbour's front garden. Parking my car towards the end of the street, which was as close as I could get, I counted the net-curtain twitches as I neared the house. Her direct neighbours had dispensed with any attempts to conceal their curiosity and were standing, feet apart, in a stance which seem to foghorn 'I have my rights' on their doorsteps.

''Scuse me, love.'

'Excuse me.'

As I reached forward to ring the bell, the photographers lifted their cameras in preparation. Inside, a quick succession of thuds could be heard – a child, surely, running too fast down the stairs. The door opened just an inch, enough to see that Gina was smiling.

'All right, love?'

As the photographers machine-gunned off their shots, I slipped inside, slamming the door shut behind me. Gina sank down on to the bottom step of the staircase, and I took in the flying ducks on the wall and the huge pile of clothes – George's – at the foot of it.

'My God.' Affecting a light pant, she looked up at me with unconcealed excitement in her eyes. 'This is crazy. C-R-A-Z-Y. I don't see why they're so interested in me.' Getting up, she pulled me by the hand into the sitting room. 'Come on, come through. George is getting dressed upstairs; he'll be down in a sec.' She smiled to herself as she spoke, and I could see the pleasure those words afforded her.

'Who is it, Mum?' came a helium screech.

'A friend of George's, munchkin,' Gina boomed back, with that rare ability a mother has to go from a whisper to a holler without ruffling her features. 'Hope you're ready up there – Vicky'll be here to pick you up and take you to your dance lesson in a second!' She turned back to me: 'I'm sorry there's no milk – what you looking at?'

I was peering through the net-curtains at the paparazzi.

'Oh – don't worry about that. Look at him, though ...' she giggled at the photographer on the slide. 'I hope he gets stuck in there for good. Actually, no I don't – Jessica likes that slide.'

'How old is she?'

'Katie's nine and Jessica's seven,' said Gina, handing me a cup with a picture of a sunglass-wearing chicken and the words 'Chick Magnate' adorning the front – a gift to her former boyfriend in happier times, I guessed. 'They're very good girls, and they have just fallen in love with George. I mean I swear,' she put her hands on those tiny, moulded hips and affected a sulky pout, 'I get quite jealous sometimes – he'll play with them for hours.'

I hadn't expected this. As far as I could tell, children seemed to inspire guilt in George, perhaps because he wished he'd spent more time with his own son.

Gina was prattling on, busy making plans like a woman with a new life ahead of her. 'How long since you last saw George?' she asked abruptly.

'A few weeks now. He—'

'You and he had a barney, didn't you?' She was standing too close, the daylight lingering on that flawless face with its elaborately made-up eyes and film star lips.

I didn't have time to answer. An ankle, tanned and swollen, had appeared at the top of the stairs: it was George. Scatty-haired and rheumy-eyed in a raspberry-coloured dressing gown – Gina's, I guessed – so short and narrow that it revealed a good six inches of shaggy chest, he held my gaze, smiling.

The hug I hadn't expected.

'Forgiven me yet?'

He breathed hot, sharp air into my face and I absorbed his features, still close, in all their detail: the ashen skin, scabbed nose and burnt yellowing around the eyes.

'Don't look so shocked.' He let his hands, reddened and chapped by psoriasis, slide from my shoulders, reawakening that curious, yeast-like smell with the movement. 'In answer to the question you haven't asked yet: yes, I have been drinking. And I'd like to clear something up now, if you and I are going to be seeing each other again after today. I'm going to keep on drinking.' He reached out and tilted my chin up, forcing me to maintain eye contact. 'I am. So you're going to have to accept that.'

Observing the scene fondly from the kitchen doorway, Gina let out a squeal, before bounding over and wrapping her arms around George's waist.

'He just wants to have some fun for a bit, don't you?'

I ignored her, addressing George: 'For how long?'

'How long do I want to have fun for?' he smirked, grappling playfully with Gina's hands.

'How long do you want to carry on drinking for? A week, a month? Until you get hospitalised again?'

He blinked at this last part, as though closing his eyes even for a fraction of a second might make it untrue.

'Just for the moment,' said his blonde ventriloquist gaily from behind him.

'For the moment,' he repeated slowly. Then he gave me the smallest of winks.

For a second, Gina's twittering, the feline curl of her body around George, standing there in that ridiculous dressing gown, and his demands for tea and toast, was drowned out. In that one tiny movement, which might have been a twitch or a trick of light, George was telling me that he had decided to kill himself, slowly, by living the only way he wanted to.

I understood him well enough by then to know that his vanity would gorge on any reaction, so I forced myself to remain blank-faced.

'And what about your contract with the paper?'

It took him a second to recover.

'You know the drill, Trouble: I need the money. And if people really do want to hear the finer points of my life as it stands, they're welcome to them. So everyone's a winner, right?' He performed a mock bow which had the effect of sending Gina on to the sofa in a giggling heap. 'Everyone's a winner.'

'And you're really happy to share this,' I gestured at him, trying not to laugh as he tugged defensively on the straining tie around his waist, 'with everyone?'

'Why not?'

A small girl in pink ran fast and low like an animal through the room to join her mother on the sofa.

'You sure about that, George? You're ready to tell people about you two,' I mouthed the last two words, conscious of the little girl.

But he was distracted by the wriggling mass of mother and daughter, advancing upon them threateningly, the kindly ogre, ready to pounce. 'What's going on over here – what is going on?'

There was no need for the pantomime, he looked sinister enough already, but the girls' shrieks – indistinguishable from one another – were filled with wild joy.

Gina extricated herself first, taking the girl, Katie – who I could see now was as pretty as her mother – upstairs to get dressed. George, breathing in shallow gulps from the exertion, went to the fridge and poured some white wine into a mug.

'Couldn't keep away, eh? Just like the rest of them.'

'Something like that.'

Batting away the debris of headless dolls, ballet leotards and jailbait clothing too small even to belong to Gina, George patted the space next to him on the sofa. We sat in silence, taking in the squeals from above and chittering of the paparazzi outside. George coddled his cup of wine like tea, while I tried to temper the question I was desperate to ask, knowing how accusatory it might sound.

'George, what is going on here?' It was the best I could do. I lowered my voice into a whisper. 'I mean, what is all this?'

He shot me a deliberately obtuse look. 'I'm happy here. Alex has made it clear that she doesn't want me and Gina looks after me. What's the problem?'

It was as though I'd missed six months or a year of his life, not a fortnight.

'But where did you go? How did you meet her?'

'Does it really matter?' He put a hand to his face and dragged the loose skin beneath his eyes down in a gesture of exhaustion. 'I just did.'

'But where?'

'The Chequers – I met her a while ago actually, at the pub.'

I closed my eyes. 'Of course.'

'It's quite a funny story, actually. I was in a scuffle with this snapper who'd been sticking his lens in my face and Gina came up afterwards to see if I was OK. Turns out I know her brother. Anyway, I was far too drunk to remember what I said but apparently it was, "You're gorgeous – fancy an affair?" Smooth, eh?'

'You've still got it, George. What woman—'

We were interrupted by the sound of Gina herding two girls down the stairs. Behind them trailed an assortment of clothes, bags and dolls. Jessica, the younger of the two, was whinnying and clinging to her mother's hip, thumb, ponytail and mouth all attached in a protective brace around her head. Katie followed, throwing a mistrustful look my way.

'I'm just going to drop them round at Vicky's next door – safer, I think,' she whispered.

'Jessica, my love,' George leaned across me strenuously, trying to catch the little girl's attention, and I could feel his heart beating fast through the dressing gown. 'Jessica, come and say goodbye.'

She did as she was told, throwing me a formal 'hello' on her way over.

'Come on, baby.' Waiting by the front door, Gina gave her hair a toss. 'See you in a bit, Georgie.'

I waited until I heard the door close.

'George – what the hell are you playing at? Two weeks ago, Alex was the love of your life and you were willing to go cold turkey, the whole lot, just to get her back. Now what? You've got yourself a whole new family?' I paused, knowing it wasn't my place to say any of this, but not caring either. 'Seriously, George. You've already got a family . . .'

Knowing that George had been on the rampage, I had prepared myself for the worst: a debauched monster who barely ate or slept, a total recluse or a frenetic drunk who had to be kicked out of the pub at closing time. I knew, from past reports, that he liked to pick up beautiful strays, especially during drinking binges, but this desire to enter into terminal decline within ordered confines, to play at domesticity while committing slow suicide, baffled me.

'Have you spoken to Alex?'

'It's all over with Alex,' he said testily. 'You know that.'

'Oh come on, George.'

I made as if to stand up, but he pulled me back down again. Turning to face me, he revealed a swathe of brown thigh.

'Avert your eyes, would you, dear?'

Gina had obviously allowed him to reclaim the cavalier persona he felt such nostalgia for.

'I don't know how she does it.'

He gestured outside, from where Gina could be heard asking, in TV phraseology, for her and George's 'privacy to be respected'.

'But I'm happy here, with her. She lets me get on with things, doesn't nag – and she's a minx.'

I knew that look: he was on the verge of giving details I had no interest in knowing.

'Don't, George.'

'Let's just say seven times a night. Jealous?'

'Horribly.'

'I think you are, too.'

'Right.' I stood up. 'We need to make a plan. How about you, me and Gina get in my car now and go somewhere safe, somewhere without all these guys on your doorstep.' I gestured towards the front garden where Gina was still taking questions. 'Maybe we pop in to the hospital on the way, where they can—'

'No!' Anger rejuvenated him for an instant. 'This is the last time I'm going to say this: I am not going to see a doctor. And if you ever so much as bring it up . . .' Gina had come back in, radiant. 'If you ever mention it again,' George concluded in a low voice, 'I will cut you out, understood? Just cut you out.'

'They're like animals out there,' Gina smiled, 'asking me all sorts about us, babe. But don't worry – I said we had no comment.'

Getting up and wrapping his arms about Gina's waist, he put those dimples to work, 'Good girl.'

'They were offering me money and all sorts – can you believe that? Ten grand this bloke from one of the Sunday tabs said he'd give me.'

But George wasn't listening. 'How about you and me take a nap, darling, and then I take you both out for a pub lunch? So that my girls can get to know each other?'

A half-remembered quote, 'Charm is a form of dishonesty,' came to me as I registered the about turn and watched them both disappear upstairs.

Three hours later we were running in one lunatic trio, eyes shielded from the flashes, to the car. Despite the recent drop in temperature, George wore only his tracksuit bottoms and a T-shirt, while Gina had changed into jeans which clung like sausage-wrap around those provocative, schoolgirl's legs. Then there was me, not for the first time that summer wondering what on earth I was doing.

The pub – an aseptic, two-floor affair – was empty; no surprise as it was two minutes to twelve. George's mood had dipped during the ten-minute drive, so that while Gina chattered on, one arm snuggled forcefully beneath his, he gazed unseeingly out of the window, nodding occasionally or throwing her the appeasing smile of a distracted parent. Perhaps he was replaying our conversation, but I thought it more likely that he was thinking about Alex, and how damned their relationship would be tomorrow morning when photographs of him and Gina together were published in the papers. He knew that letting go of his wife was severing that last link to normality, definitively renouncing any idea of containing his addiction.

'A diet coke and a Pinot Grigio, please. And you, Celia – what'll you have?' We were at the upstairs bar and Gina was bouncing gently on her tiptoes at the bar, every muscle in her curvy little body tensed.

Drinks in hand, George wandered over to the open balustraded circle in the centre of the room, and looked down into the bar below.

'I'll make sure none of them journalists get in here and start bothering you, all right, Mr Best?' the barman shouted over ingratiatingly. 'Just you grab a table in that corner and you'll be more comfortable. If you like,' he winked, pleased with himself, 'we could put your wine in a Coke can or a coffee mug – just in case?'

George ignored both offers, settling himself at a table in the centre of the room, and gestured to Gina and me to seat ourselves, harem-like, on either side of him.

'Doesn't get much better than this, eh?' Arms outstretched along our chair tops, he looked from me to Gina and back again. 'I've got my sitter on one side and,' he turned and slipped a hand under Gina's top, exposing a few inches of skin, 'and my beauty queen on the other.'

Gina beamed.

'Do you know,' he said, observing his own hand as it travelled up, a friendly rodent beneath her sweatshirt, 'that in a few weeks' time I'll get my decree nisi?' More lies. 'Do you know what that means, Gina?'

'Course I know what that means.' From the thinning of her lips I saw that George had offended her, and I liked her the more for it.

'It means,' he explained, wrinkling up his nose and snickering softly into her face as though she were an infant, he explained, 'that I'll be a single man. On the market . . .'

I imagined George as a commodity; something you could actively pick out from the shop shelf, and the idea that anyone would find something so damaged desirable made me laugh out loud.

'Hey! What?'

'Nothing – just that you'll be bloody lucky if anyone is willing to have you the way you're going.'

He grinned and pulled his hand out from beneath Gina's top. 'Fair point – you could say that I'm not perfect husband material.'

Even Gina had the good grace to laugh at that one. 'All right then: you're not perfect husband material.'

'So, I remember this one time with my first wife,' George's voice had increased in volume and the barman looked up from slicing his limes, 'I told her I was popping out for a drink and came back six weeks later. Forgot to mention it would be in Barcelona.'

Gina shrieked with laughter and slapped the table.

'Seriously though,' he took a long draught of wine and paused for a moment to luxuriate in the feel of it, 'she just didn't get it.'

'Women can be funny about their husbands drinking themselves to death,' I cut in.

'It's true. She couldn't handle it, whereas Alex used to go through stages of trying to get me to stop, but every now and again she would see that I was on a mission and just let me be. She knew me well enough to understand when it was useless.'

Every time George mentioned Alex, Gina's face snapped shut – not that George had noticed. Gesturing to the barman for another round, he went on: 'She adopted the damage limitation approach early on, giving me these tablets to clean out my liver and cooking me comfort food.' He paused. 'I did AA once, did you know that?'

I knew this story – he was telling it for Gina's benefit.

'I managed a whole twenty days there. Twenty days – can you imagine? They even gave me a frigging medal, but I loathed every minute of it. No, no.' He held a hand, flat as a paddle, up in the air. 'No, that's not true: those first five minutes, when I had to stand up in front of a dozen people and say, "Hi, I'm George Best and I'm an alcoholic ..." ' His jowls were shuddering with laughter and the yellowed whites of his eyes were glossy with tears. 'The look on those peoples' faces was enough to make it worthwhile. Oh,' up went the volume again, 'and actually there turned out to be one very pretty girl there ...'

I examined Gina's face for more signs of jealousy, but there were none – just the rapt focus of a religious fanatic. Anything was acceptable; this was all part of the George Best mythology.

'Tried it on but she wasn't having any of it – something about us being bad for each other.'

He and Gina fell together in a hysterical clinch, and the last strains of my disapproval fell away. In their different ways, both George and Gina had had a rough side, yet both generated some kind of natural warmth that it was hard to remain immune to. The pair probably weren't good for one another, but that afternoon I tried to suspend all judgement.

Besides, I was tired of the matronly role I had fallen into. Technically, I was here to make sure George stayed faithful to the paper he was contracted to, and that was it.

'It's all cyclical with George,' Phil had once said. 'So remember that however mad things become you can always predict what the next stage will be: the guilt kicks in, he gets sick of treating his body like a punchbag, and that's when he gets started on the "comeback".'

He knew George better than anyone, but I had begun to wonder whether alcoholism, like a person, matures and transmutes. It's been said that there are two kinds of drunks: the marathon drinkers and the slow and destructive alcoholics – although some, like Richard Burton and George, would morph from one to the other during the course of their lifetimes. It appeared that my charge might be entering a third stage, and yet I hoped Phil would be proved right, and that this premeditated binge, the kamikaze drinking and the affair with Gina was just a reaction to Alex's divorce proceedings. Perhaps, when the end of his marriage was close enough to touch, he would pull back from the brink.

George and Gina had dissolved into a noisy embrace and I sat, fingering my straw, avoiding the barman's eye.

'George,' came a muffled reprimand from beneath him, 'it's rude . . .'

'Rude?' he pulled himself upright and looked over at me, his chin and the stubbled skin above his mouth sticky and lightly glittered with Gina's lip gloss.

'You feeling left out?' he leered.

'I am.'

As from the first day spent with George, I hadn't touched a drop of alcohol. Yet the relentlessness of his drinking and their flirting soon had me feeling light-headed. It was a Saturday and both floors had started filling with regulars, families and men escaping their wives and girlfriends to meet for illicit drinks. There had been a few, scarcely dissimulated stares at our table, the usual, audible whispers of 'George Best – it is, isn't it?' and two requests for autographs. At some point, the outsized TV screen to the right of the bar had been switched on and a cluster of men had reorganised their chairs around it accordingly.

George's eyes flickered up to the game – Manchester United were playing – from time to time, but he was far more interested in Gina, who had covered the table in an elabo-rate pattern of Smarties prised from the sweet machine in the corner. George had kept up the tales, both sad and funny, of the attempts he and others had made to stop the drinking.

'I even tried aversion therapy once, years and years ago – know what that is?' He had addressed this question to Gina.

She shook her head.

'It's when you surround yourself with the thing that you love, the thing you're addicted to, in the hope that it'll eventually turn you off it.' Gina nodded, granting him a smile steeped in idolatry. 'Only this time it was my idea. I got it from Richard Harris.' He looked at Gina's blank face and threw his hands up in despair. 'The actor – you do know who Richard Harris is, right?'

She blinked woozily, and he stopped talking long enough to empty his glass. One of George's keenest pleasures, I had learned, was to keep people waiting, mid-anecdote, while he finished a drink.

'I'd read that Harris had tried aversion therapy: filled every room and every cupboard of his house with bottles of vodka. It worked apparently, though not for long, so I thought I'd give it a go. I went down to my local off-licence at the time, and I bought the place up.'

People had started angling their heads towards our table, intent on catching the tale's punch line.

'I picked up two dozen bottles of vodka and enough white wine to kill a man.'

Neither Gina nor I could resist a splutter of laughter.

'You should have seen the looks on the shop assistants' faces – I reckon they thought that was my weekly stash or something. And when the neighbours saw it all being unloaded I reckon they thought I'd finally lost it.'

'And?' Gina had one hand over her mouth. 'Did it work?'

The room fell silent, the match ignored as people strained to hear his answer.

'Did it hell. I'd put bottles of wine in the bathroom cabinet, the vodka on top of the TV and stuffed the fridge so full of alcohol that there was no place for food, and you know what happened? Within a couple of days I'd hoovered up every last drop. So much for aversion therapy.'

Those who had been listening in were now laughing openly, as was Gina. I wondered whether the story was even true or not, or whether it was one of George's fun stories, designed to entertain.

'You're a nutter,' she announced, pulling George in by the neck and giving him a kiss.

People were no longer bothering to disguise their stares. Manchester United were losing, and there had been a subtle but perceptible shift in the atmosphere. Was it my imagination or were those eyes not quite as benevolent as they had been? Bursts of dismay erupted and we all looked up: Manchester United had just ceded the winning goal. A cluster of men got up and wandered, truculent and swearing, to the bar.

'They say you should never meet your idols – and you're living proof of that, ain't you?' A red-haired man nearing fifty had appeared out of nowhere.

'Why's that?' George asked politely.

''Cause you haven't been a footballer for a long time, have you, mate? You're just a pisshead who's always been more interested in the next drink and the next lay than anything else.'

He gestured towards Gina and me with his pint, guzzled a mouthful and, sucking the foam from his top lip, stared insolently at George.

'I think we're all agreed there.' George gazed unflinchingly back at him. 'What, exactly, would you like me to do about it?'

'It'd be nice if you were a better role model to the lads, eh?' This guy wasn't going to let it go. 'Don't you think?

George Best is the greatest, the *best* footballer that ever lived – that's what we're told. Well, I don't buy it.'

George had locked eyes with the man, pausing only to take tiny sips of wine, as though objectively mulling over the points raised.

'The way I see it,' continued the man, risking a quick glance at Gina's crossed legs, 'you're just someone who missed out on being the world's best footballer by becoming the world's biggest arsehole instead.'

Because of what had happened in Malta and that last day at Forest Mere, I was able – albeit too late – to predict what happened next, but still it made me jump. George had leapt, agile as a teenager, from his seat and bent the man over the balustrade so that his head was dangling upside down into the bar below. Although smaller than him by at least a foot, George was stronger and had managed to bend one of the man's arms behind his back while forcing his head down still further.

'Say that again, mate?' The veins in George's arms, fish green, protruded like old wiring.

'You're a fucking lunatic,' the man gurgled into the abyss. 'Get the fuck off me.'

The room had been silenced, but a constant drone, jarring in its joviality, from those as yet unaware of the scene taking place above them, drifted up from downstairs.

I thought then, quite calmly, that this would be how the whole thing would end. George would seriously hurt this man, go to prison and that would be that. I thought of the headlines and, inappropriately, of what the office would say. Then I wondered whether he would be able to get hold of any drink inside. I must have closed my eyes, because when I looked again the man was pulling himself off the floor by a chair leg and George was pouring himself another glass of wine.

A little way off, Gina looked up from examining the heel of her shoe and smiled. 'Boys, eh?'

It had taken ten minutes for the coffee machine in my Holiday Inn room to dribble out the half-cup of murky water I sat warming my hands with, waiting for the clock to strike 7 a.m., so that I could call the office.

That the previous afternoon's events hadn't made it into that day's papers was some consolation, but I was pleased that I had warned the desk just in case. Ever since George had resurfaced, the paper seemed to be losing its claim on him and stories about his disintegration, with ever more lurid and compelling details, had been filling the pages of our competitors.

'This is going to start happening more and more now,' my boss had sighed when I recounted the incident. 'In fact, he probably gets into a fight pretty much every time he goes out now, right?'

'Probably,' I agreed.

'Did he cause any damage to the pub?'

'No – actually they apologised to him and threw the other guy out . . .'

'That makes sense . . . But, look, he can't be in these places, doing what he does any more. We're playing a different game now. We're dealing with a man who has nothing to lose.'

'So . . .' I felt weary. I'd been absent from my life too long to have any points of references left. 'What do you suggest?'

'We get him away from this Gina woman, preferably back to Forest Mere or Alex, who at least keeps him in check.'

'Alex is not going to have him back, not after he moved his stuff into Gina's. Besides, he's really keen on Gina – and Forest Mere didn't exactly work for him last time, did it?'

'Still, it might be the safest option. Get Phil to help you out with this; nobody's going to be giving George any work if he's beating people up – including us.'

'I don't know,' I said, uncertain. 'He seems pretty ensconced. She really looks after him, and it's been going on far longer than I thought – before he even went to Malta, I think. He seems to be enjoying this perfect family unit he's accumulated.'

'Tough.' I could hear typing starting up again in the background, a sign that, for all intents and purposes, the conversation was over.

'Oh, and another thing: Gina's getting all kinds of offers for her story. The *News of the World* has offered her twenty grand.'

The typing stopped.

'We'll get Gina to a safe house, tell her it's best for her and for George, and that they can be together again in time . . .'

'Wait – Gina?'

'Gina's the key to this whole mess now: we need to make sure nobody else gets to her. You speak to Phil, tell him what George got up to last night, let him take care of that side, and I'll get the safe house sorted out now. We'll text you with the details and where to pick up the money.'

'Money?'

'You'll be needing some money to pay for the house – I don't want our landlady to start getting curious so best to pay in cash.'

I took a sip of my tepid coffee. 'What about the kids?'

A sigh of frustration. 'Can Gina leave them with a neighbour or something?'

'I doubt she'll want to. How long are we going to do this thing for?'

'I don't know.' I could tell by the tetchiness in his voice that the children were an unwelcome addition to the whole tableau. 'Look, this woman's getting her fifteen minutes – I'm presuming that's what she's in it for – right?'

CHAPTER SEVEN

'I STILL DON'T UNDERSTAND WHY, though.'

Gina was sitting on her living room floor, a St Trinian-like figure in a pleated miniskirt, electric blue knickers just visible within the shadows of her crossed legs. Arched over her smooth brown knees in an ecstasy of sensual feline indulgence was her youngest child, Jessica, who had pulled her vest up to her neck and was guiding her mother's hands past the hazy smudges of her nipples down to her tummy.

'There, Mum, there.'

Gina looked from me to her daughter for a second. 'Does it hurt?'

'No,' Jessica curled her toes with impatience. 'Tickle it, Mummy, tickle.'

Gina's fingers did their work distractedly.

'Where is this place, anyway?'

'About an hour and a bit's drive away, in West Sussex, but the girls will be quite safe there. The house looks beautiful and there's a big garden. You girls would like that, wouldn't you?'

'Course they would.' It was the first thing George, lying

on the sofa with a glass of wine in his hands, had said since I'd got there. He was smiling but his eyes were bloodshot and his stomach swollen like a toddler's beneath his T-shirt. Jessica had removed the sock from one of his feet and was inspecting his big toe with an expression of delighted disgust.

'It would give them a nice holiday before they have to go back to school. And maybe it wouldn't be such a bad thing for you to escape these bloodsuckers for a couple of days, Gina.'

Phil, I deduced, had given him a talking-to.

Jessica, bored of his toe, followed the grown-ups' eye line to the window, where nebulous outlines of men, less than a foot away from the net-curtained window, could be made out. Only Gina had no reason or desire to flee from the press, and would never come willingly with me if she thought that George was being taken away from her.

'Then, in a couple of days, when things have died down a bit, George could come and join us down there, couldn't you, George?'

He nodded, raising an eyebrow when Gina wasn't looking, to make it clear that he knew my game.

'So you'd join us there by the weekend?' Gina bit her lip fetchingly, and I knew that the hardest part was over.

When we crept out of the house at 6.30 a.m. the following day, there was no sign of life outside. Even the most tenacious doorstepper – a lanky young man I recognised from Malta who had tried desperately to extract a few words from George as he had left with Phil late the previous night – was asleep in his car, face smeared against the window, feet propped up on a dashboard cluttered with KFC wrappers. The girls had dozed off immediately, but Gina was too excited to sleep, and in a feverish whisper asked question after question: would the girls each have a room of their own? And would there be a washing machine, only she'd packed a big pile of clothes she hadn't had time to take to the launderette. Demands, little and precise as pinpricks, perforated her sentences. The girls would need new swimming costumes, of course, for sunbathing – would the paper be paying for those? I agreed to everything, conscious that what I had presented to her and the girls as a blissful country break had the potential to feel more like incarceration once the novelty had worn off – certainly when it became clear that George would not be joining them.

Leaving those warm bodies misting the windows in the car park at Gatwick, where an envelope of cash was waiting for me at a money desk, I experienced a moment of trepidation so strong that it stopped me, mid-jog. Babysitting George made some kind of sense; minding these girls (even though she was older than I was, Gina always seemed like a girl to me) who played no part in the grander scheme of things, lying to them, didn't feel good. I thought about what a veteran journalist friend would say: that if I weren't doing this, Gina would align herself with another newspaper which would take her away to a safe house, just as I was doing now. To those outside the media, these would sound like dubious ethics, but they helped temper the cramps of conscience that were a part of the job.

Returning a few minutes later with a fat brown paper envelope containing £2,000 – more, I hoped, than we would be needing – I was relieved to find the girls still asleep. Gina, however, was more alert than ever. Eyeing my package with wary fascination, she waited a few minutes until we were back on the motorway before whispering: 'That the money?'

'Yup.'

'Mind if I have a look?'

I handed over the envelope, and we both laughed.

Turning into the narrow gravel path signposted 'Willow Cottage' an hour and a half later, my worries lifted slightly. It was nearly eight in the morning and the sky, split into Turner-like washes of iridescent colour, lit up a large, renovated Tudor cottage behind the set of sturdy wooden gates. It was the start of another hot September day from that interminable, broiling summer, of the kind we haven't seen since, and Gina, more excited and awake than the rest of us, had leapt from the car to throw the gates open before we had even ground to a standstill.

'We there?' Jessica yawned from the back seat.

'Yes, we are. Girls,' I shook a pink-socked foot, unsure whom it belonged to, 'wake up.'

Katie's face, swollen by sleep, surfaced.

It took the girls fifteen minutes to locate the cupboard beneath the stairs, which was rammed full of bicycles, skipping ropes, defunct footballs and pogo sticks left behind by past inhabitants. Their mother, meanwhile, moved from room to room in a trance, occasionally stopping to finger the flounce of a curtain or a Staffordshire dog's paw with a perfect split of delight and mistrust. Concerns about the girls having to share a room were unfounded. There were four bedrooms on the top floor, two of them perfect in size and décor (both different shades of pink) for Jessica and Katie. The master bedroom, a low-ceilinged room shaded,

I suspected, throughout the day by the overhang of thatch from above, and decorated with William Morris wallpaper, had sent Gina into peels of delight. Kicking off her flip-flops she had bounced on the four-poster bed until I feared it might break.

'Just wait until I tell George about this. I'm telling you – he'll be down here before you know it.'

I had thought the days at Willow Cottage would drag by, that as the only one who knew we weren't allowed to leave, I would feel suffocated, but a week passed quickly in a cycle of domestic practicalities. Gina was a good mother, being little more than a child herself, and every day began and ended with an orgy of female petting. I couldn't decide whether, had George been present, he would have luxuriated in the stifling female rule of the house or fled, emasculated, from it. With the studied nonchalance of pre-sexual girls, Gina had taken to walking around the house in knickers, rolled down low on her hips and barely covering that brown bottom. She seemed to specialise in finding degrees of nakedness where I had believed there were only absolutes. Every new combination had been covered, I assumed, until the morning she walked into my bedroom wearing nothing but a shower cap, complaining that there were no clean towels. Following me to the airing cupboard where I handed her one from the pile I'd folded away the day before, I noted with interest that the emotion on her face was uncomplicated pride. Her nakedness wasn't designed to embarrass, excite or threaten: it was a single perfect thing she was proud of.

'Thank you,' she trilled, padding off down the hall.

At first, when George was phoning every day, sending

Gina skitting off into corners, all low murmurs and high-pitched laughter, everyone seemed content. Then came the first day he didn't call. On the second, Gina changed her nail colour twice; on the third, she announced that it might be time to get the kids back and ready for the new term.

'I mean where is he? He hasn't ...' She covered her mouth with an iridescent blue-tipped hand, sure, suddenly, of something. 'Has he called you? He has, hasn't he?'

'No.' And he hadn't. 'Honestly, Gina. He hasn't.'

I did know from the news desk, however, that George had been at Forest Mere since the day we left, 'getting himself back on track' – and that meant away from Gina. I knew too that today was the day Alex had agreed to join him there for those long-postponed 'talks', despite being pictured yesterday (much to Gina's satisfaction) without her wedding ring.

Looking at me as though I had all the answers, she asked, 'Do you think he's with her? Do you think she's trying to get him back?'

Given her role in the scenario, I found her rancour towards Alex inexplicable. It jarred too, with her naturally warm disposition.

'I really don't know, Gina. Sorry ...'

'Because if he does go back to her, I might ... I mean, I think that would be ...' She was gearing up for something and I didn't know what. 'I mean that would change everything. It would mean that the man who keeps calling me was right: George was just stringing me along, and ...'

'Which man?'

'The one I told you about.' She concentrated on pushing down a cuticle to avoid looking at me. 'You know, the one who offered me twenty grand for my story. They've upped it to twenty-five, actually,' she added faintly. 'Not that I'd ever take the money.'

Had I understood just how fragile Gina's mindset was, I would have had the foresight to hide the papers the following morning.

She gave me a shock, crumpled over the kitchen table like that, knees hunched into her chest, the papers spread out with forensic precision on the table before her.

'Gina,' I put a hand to her head. 'It's seven in the morning – why are you up so early?'

I ran my hand evenly along that platinum mane, knowing what must have happened and trying to think ahead, find appeasing phrases that might somehow help.

'George is a little bastard,' she said, ignoring my question and looking up at me miserably. 'Look!'

In matching bathrobes on the balcony of his room at Forest Mere, bodies interacting with the fresh flirtation born of a reunion, George and Alex looked like honeymooners. The image was sharp, too sharp even for those long lenses, and I wondered whether it had been set up by Alex – or George, perhaps. Either way, it was a beautifully choreographed and unmistakable message to Gina that their dalliance had ended the way of all the others. Alex may be the beleaguered wife, but he would always, in the end, go back to her.

Cursing myself for George's continued ability to surprise me, I busied myself with making tea.

'Do you think she's pretty?'

Bent so far forward over the page that the strap of satin slip she wore slid from her shoulder, her head to one side, Gina was scrutinising a picture of Alex, as though finding some new angle might tell her how she measured up.

'I suppose,' I'd replied meekly, avoiding the look of betrayal in her eyes.

'I think she's too thin. And cold-looking,' she announced with authority. 'She's not a man's woman.' Gina nodded to herself, confirming her own beliefs and comforted, for a second at least, by the knowledge that, for all the happiness it had brought her, she was exactly that.

'Maybe you're right.' I was worried by how badly she was taking this, aware that I needed to find a way to brighten her mood. 'So what do you want to do today?'

'I think I should wake the girls and we can drive over there,' she rejoined crisply. 'Find out what's really going on and bring him back here. If he won't come back to me,' her eyes darkened, 'then I might just give that journalist a call. George promised he'd look after me and the girls, you know. He promised. He also said I would never have to worry about anything again. How am I meant to get by now?'

'Gina, calm down. I know what you're thinking, but if you do that interview George might never speak to you again. Is that what you want?'

Not having thought that far ahead, she looked crestfallen.

'I just know that I could tell them a thing or two about him, about how he treats women. And I've got proof: I've kept the sheets from our first night together,' she added triumphantly. 'I haven't washed them or anything.'

'Gina,' I tried to keep my voice steady. 'What are you talking about? Wash the sheets for God's sake. This isn't the

OJ Simpson trial. And anyway, whatever you say George can easily deny if he wants to, whatever "evidence" you have, it'll just be your word against his.'

'You think?' She was pointlessly desirable in her silk slip. 'Yes . . . maybe you're right.'

'She did *what*?'

It was rare to hear astonishment in my boss's voice, there being few of life's perversities he hadn't already come across.

'So we're dealing with a mad woman.' He said this matter-of-factly. 'Which makes it all the more important for you to keep her there, away from George, who might have a hope in hell of making it to Christmas if he stays with Alex, and away from the press. Is the *News of the World* still on her tail?'

'Yes.'

'Great.'

'Can I just ask,' I wasn't sure why I cared, 'who is with George?'

'Hmmm?' My boss had mentally moved on to something else. 'We've sent a reporter from the news desk to keep an eye on him.'

'Wouldn't it be best to swap us over? I mean Gina might respond better to a man and I'm starting to feel pretty bad about her.'

'No, we're keeping things as they are. You've built up a relationship with this woman, and God knows hers is the most newsworthy story right now.' These words might have jarred a month ago; now they seemed acceptable – even normal. 'If it all goes horribly wrong with George,' he went on, 'we may need her exclusive.'

'Oh, Christ.' I was in my bedroom, and Gina had just walked in. 'Well, let me know if you do hear from him, won't you?' I turned to Gina. 'Alex's mum,' I explained quickly, stuffing my phone back into my bag. 'I just wanted to see what was going on; whether those pictures meant anything.'

'And?'

'She didn't want to tell me anything.'

'I've been calling his mobile all day and he won't pick up . . .'

'You know he never uses it.'

'I thought maybe you could try calling . . . Alex?'

It was at once a wrench and a perverse pleasure for Gina to say her name. She lingered over the word with the same gratification a woman gets from the methodical examination of a sexual competitor.

'I don't think that would be a good idea. I don't want them to feel hounded. If he is back with her,' and there was no doubt in my mind that he was, 'I'd rather leave them to it, Gina.' Maybe all she needed was a little honesty. 'She is his wife and we can't force him to do anything he doesn't want to do.'

I felt the hypocrisy of my words so strongly that I had to turn my face away, but Gina was too caught up in her own jealousy to notice.

'I know he loves me. He said so and, I mean, it was obvious, wasn't it?'

Gina spent the rest of that day ricocheting between supreme confidence and wild insecurity. In between working out ways to get hold of George which wouldn't be frustrated by Alex, replaying whole conversations with her lover and making embarrassingly explicit allusions to their sexual games, there hadn't been time for much else. The girls, not having been told that 'Uncle George' may not be coming back, played disconsolately outside, conscious that something was wrong.

'You've seen us together – what do you think?'

But she didn't want the truth. In her heart, Gina must have known that the affair she had been living out with George couldn't last. As I murmured reassurances, something George had once told me remained at the forefront of my mind. 'Do you know,' he laughingly confided, 'that as I'm sleeping with a woman, while we're in the act, I'm already tailoring how the relationship will end?'

I finally got hold of George in his room at Forest Mere later that afternoon. It was nearly six, and Alex was having a massage before dinner.

'I missed the dogs,' was the first thing he said. 'I can never go long without seeing them.'

'And Alex, George, isn't this about her?'

'Course ... she ...' He lowered his voice to a whisper. 'She's stuck with me throughout everything. She'd be a saint to give me another chance. We've talked things through, and I've told her that the whole Gina thing was rubbish made up by the papers.'

It never stopped amazing me what a natural liar he was, convincing even himself.

'But she's not wearing her wedding ring and she's been on the phone to her solicitors from the moment she got here. She goes on at me about these women, but you know what? I reckon she's fucking someone else ...'

The swearing was proof that George was still drinking,

that he had kept, unswerving, to his tacit mission, this most recent attempt at drying out being just another sham.

'I don't believe that for a second. And back to Gina, George – the "love of your life" as she tells me you call her.'

'Jesus ...'

I knew how much he hated having his own words thrown back at him. Having spent years making violent proclamations for effect, he felt he should be granted immunity from truth, or consistency. For a moment, perhaps because I was now used to the filmic volatility of his life, I had the absurd thought that he might slam the phone down, but I heard only a long exhalation.

'You of all people know that I talk bollocks 90 per cent of the time.'

We both laughed. For a moment, everything except our friendship evaporated.

'The girls miss you. Katie does your accent to a tee ...'

He laughed, but the tension in his voice was still there. 'Does she?'

I had expected to be more angry on their account; instead I felt relieved. As good as he was with the girls, he was hardly a sane person to have around.

'I never did understand how you found it so easy to be with them,' I added quietly.

'Because of Calum, you mean?' His voice had become indistinct, as though he were moving his mouth away from the phone.

'Yes. I thought it might make you want to spend more time with him, remind you that—'

He cut in, so close to the receiver now that I could hear the whistle of his saliva as he spoke.

'Shall I tell you the problem with your own kids? They're the only real reason there is to stop drinking.'

Having spotted me on the phone from outside, where she had been sunbathing as the girls danced, simian-like, around her, Gina now stood, pathetically expectant, in front of me.

'Breathe, Gina, for God's sake,' I laughed, hoping a little humour might wipe the look of dread from her face.

'Tell me. Please. I can take it. He's gone back to her, hasn't he?' She was very beautiful in her swimsuit, a few tendrils of hair clinging to her neck like ivy.

I sat down. 'He's with her, yes.'

Gina lowered her head into her hands in a way that would have been comic had it not been so genuine.

'I knew it; it's what that reporter said.'

My sympathy disappeared in an instant. 'He's called you today?'

'Three or four times,' she burst out, swallowing back tears. 'He's left all these messages, telling me that George is back with Alex, that I'm not the first woman he's done this to and that I've got a right to tell my side of the story.'

The girls were still playing outside, and I reached out and put an arm around her, feeling deep spasms shake her vertebrae through the Lycra.

'What else did he say, Gina?'

'Thirty grand,' she looked up at me. 'That's what they're offering now.'

I paused. George wasn't coming back: of course she should take the money.

'He'd feel completely betrayed if you did that, Gina. I don't know what it would do to him.'

I had said it to stop the crying, because I didn't want the girls to see her in that state. But most of all I had said it because I knew it was the only way to keep her there.

'Why? Did he say something?'

'He said he missed you,' I felt my cheeks redden with the lie, 'and the girls.'

'Did he?' She put her hands to her face, as though suddenly aware of how unkempt she looked.

'Yes, so please try and hold it together for another day or two until we hear from him.'

That night the temperature dropped five degrees. Summer was over, and the following day's papers were splattered with 'will they won't they' articles about George and Alex.

Sitting beside one another in the kitchen, bored, fed up and wondering what on earth we were doing there, Gina and I worked our way through the wildly differing stories the papers had to offer. Licking a finger before turning a page, Gina looked up at me.

'I think I'm pregnant,' she said.

CHAPTER EIGHT

WHEN PEOPLE EXPECT A strong reaction it's sometimes tempting to downplay things: take your time
before replying, keep your expression impassive. In this
case, it was impossible. My bottom lip lagged, as though
the muscles holding it in place had failed, and I was aware
that I had stopped blinking. Gina, on the other hand, was
a picture of nonchalance. Sitting back, she observed me
curiously.

'Are you OK?'

'Yes,' I stammered. 'Of course. Just a bit surprised, that's
all. But you ... when did you ... Are you sure?'

'I think so, yes.'

She got up. Maybe it was the sudden mania of movement: the filling of the kettle, and arrangement of cups and
teaspoons in their saucers that brought on my suspicions.

'How late are you?'

'A week. No, nearly ten days.'

'And you and George, you weren't ... You weren't
careful.'

'Well, you know George.' I'd never seen Gina blush before

and yet I could see the blood rising in swatches beneath her tan. 'He doesn't care about that stuff.'

We were both silent, and I wondered whether she really was naïve enough to think that this baby, if there was one, would bring George back. Some noise overhead, a bird nesting in the thatch, broke the stasis and I smiled.

'Don't you think we had better find out for sure?'

The girls, ill equipped for the change in temperature, had borrowed our jumpers and lagged behind us through a pedestrian precinct in Chichester town centre, slowed by the weight of boredom and grown-up clothing. Waiting for Gina outside the chemist earlier, I had experienced a stab of guilt when I had caught them staring enviously at a group of schoolchildren amassed on a bench outside McDonald's. We had taken them out of their lives for too long. Surely now, whatever the outcome of this test, we should all be allowed to go home.

'You going to be much longer, Gina? The girls are getting hungry.'

She had been in the changing room of a vast clothing store for nearly ten minutes, trying on a pair of jeans spotted in the shop's window on our way back to the car.

'Nearly done.' Her face, flustered and unhappy above a curtain pulled to the chin, appeared at the opening of one of the booths. 'Too bloody tight. All the biscuits I've been eating hanging around in that house.'

Perhaps it was that, along with her nervousness about the test which made her so short-tempered on the way home. Never having once heard her raise her voice to the girls, I had been surprised to hear her reprimand them both for squabbling in the back seat.

'That's enough! All I can hear is you two. Now just stop it.'

Bar the odd shuddering sniff from Jessica, the rest of the journey took place in silence.

When we got back, the girls went to their rooms immediately, slamming their respective doors in protest at the way they'd been treated. Gina kicked off her flip-flops and disappeared into the sitting room. A second later, I heard the TV erupt at full blast.

Feeling, again, that I'd been assigned the role of reigning adult, I gave Gina a few minutes before wandering into the room with two cups of tea.

She sat, her eyes fixed on the screen, apparently engrossed in an American soap opera.

I cleared my throat. 'You not curious to know, Gina?'

'Not really. No.'

This, I hadn't expected.

'Really?'

I waited.

'Are you scared of what the test will say?'

This piqued her.

'No! No.'

When she finally turned to look at me, I saw that she'd been crying.

'Shit, I've been through worse stuff than this, trust me.'

A perfume advert featuring a model Gina was frequently compared to came on and she waited for it to finish before saying anything more.

'Look, I've been thinking, and I'm not sure I want to know right now. I'm not sure I'm ready,' she added nonsensically.

'Gina …' I was annoyed now. Picking up the remote from the coffee table I turned the TV off. 'This isn't something you can ignore. Either you're pregnant or you're not. And if you are,' I persevered, 'he will need to know. Any father would need to know.'

'I'm not doing it.' The TV went back on. 'Just drop it.'

I could hear my colleagues now, picture their faces as the headline 'George Best's Love Child' was revealed in any newspaper but ours.

'Gina,' standing in between her and the television, I softened my voice. 'You have got to do this. You owe it to George.'

'Oh, Jesus.' Her toes twitched in annoyance. 'Why do you keep going on about this? What goes on with George and me is our business – mine actually, considering he's buggered off. Anyone would think it was you that was bloomin' pregnant.'

I crouched down, looking imploringly up at her. 'If I was …' I was struggling to make myself understood. 'Not that I know, of course, but if I suspected I might be pregnant …'

I stopped. Gina had fixed wide, cover-girl eyes on mine, the corners of her mouth itching to smile.

'Oh!' she said in a delighted whisper. Maybe I wouldn't have taken it further if she hadn't prompted me to.

'The truth is that I'm worried,' I began, egged on by her slow nods. 'The last time I saw my boyfriend, before we broke up, well, we were stupid.'

She was smiling now, boldly, a sympathetic hand wound around my neck. There was nothing, I suspected, Gina liked better than a female dilemma.

'Why didn't you say so? You've been worried all this time, and not said anything?'

'Not massively,' I backtracked, conscious that, even in the lunacy of the past few months, this was breaking new territory. 'It's probably just stress; I'm sure it must be. Or an unfamiliar setting – all that.' And yet this would be one way around things, maybe the only way to be sure that she was telling the truth.

'There are two of those things, aren't there?' I had seen the box in its bag on the hall table. 'How about we do one each, eh?' I injected a low laugh, to cover me in case she refused. 'At least it would put our minds at rest.'

Gina laughed along with me, releasing her hand from my neck and running it nervously through her hair. Was that fear or shiftiness in her eyes?

'You think we should?'

'Why not?' I shrugged. 'At least we'll be going through the whole thing together.'

Ten minutes later, the unused pregnancy test in the downstairs lavatory bin, I sat with my back against the door and my knees pulled into my chest charting the sluggish progress of a drop of water down the porcelain basin stand. When it reached the bottom, disappearing under a crack in the linoleum, I headed upstairs to find Gina.

Sitting on the side of the bath, legs crossed, she had the expectant, powerless air of a passenger waiting for her journey to start. Her nervousness, it struck me, was all too authentic. There was nothing simulated about the tapping of her foot on the floor or the way she scratched away at her nail varnish, peeling off great flakes and flicking them into the basin.

'How long's it been?'

'Not yet a minute. You?'

'Oh. False alarm. I feel a bit stupid now . . .'

'No don't – that's good, right?'

'Right.'

She leaned over to examine the plastic stick lying on the end of the bath.

'One line.'

'We need two, remember?'

'Oh, yeah.'

'Hear that rustling noise?'

Strains of the girls' bossy voices as they played in the garden permeated the silence, but there was something closer – a rustling above us.

Gina didn't answer.

'It's mice, I think, they get into the thatch, apparently, to keep warm.'

She looked so forlorn, that I wondered for the first time since breakfast whether she really might be pregnant. That, or, in some semi-fantasy, genuinely believe that she was. Two and a half minutes had passed and, feeling cramp set into my calf, I peered over at the test. It was unchanged.

'You're all right, Gina. We're both all right.'

She was silent, biting her lip.

'To be honest, I never really believed I might be. Did you?'

'Yes.'

At length she spoke. 'I think it's too early to tell, but I'm going to go and see the doctor next week to find out for sure.'

Again, I thought it possible that she was deluded. I wanted to feel sympathetic, reach out and take her hand, but the whole episode had caused me to wonder how much of what she was telling me was true.

'Maybe. Still, we've done all we can for the moment. Come on, Gina.' I looked over at her hunched figure, the sympathy I had tried to rouse earlier finally making itself felt. 'Let's go and see what the girls are up to.'

She didn't move.

'Gina. It wouldn't have helped things – if you were pregnant, I mean.' Not knowing what the truth was, I didn't want to accuse her, unfairly of lying. 'It wouldn't have made George come back, you know.'

She nodded, standing up a little unsteadily and running her index fingers beneath her eyes in a gesture of perfect symmetry.

'I know. You're right,' she nodded demurely. 'But do you know what? I think I'd like to take the girls home now.'

Gina kept up this show of serenity until we reached Ewell. A cluster of journalists were waiting on her doorstep. To judge by the outfit she had changed into before we left West Wittering – a hot pink, off-the-shoulder top and denim miniskirt – she'd anticipated this.

'You still with George, Gina?'

'How d'you feel about him now?'

'What about Alex, Gina?'

'Come on.' Taking hold of her arm, I guided her quickly past them, ushering the girls into the house, but it was too late, she had turned back.

'They're back together, aren't they?' she asked nobody

in particular, as the pack rattled off their pictures. Then, throwing her arms open wide, she said, 'I mean, where would you boys rather be?'

'I think you know what I'm going to say,' my boss said, with the briefest of smiles.

'What's he done now?'

'He's ready to talk about happened with Alex at Forest Mere.'

A report on the day of my return to London claimed that George had tried to throttle Alex when challenged about Gina. The resulting scene had been so impassioned that Forest Mere security had been forced to intercede. Having come to expect these violent scenes as part of the hysteria of George's life, I hadn't been surprised. I did wonder, however, along with the rest of the country, why these two refused to cut one another loose.

Gina had rung the second she read the piece, at half past seven in the morning – only not as exultant as I'd thought she might be.

'You've seen the papers?'

'Yes – I don't believe a word of it. George would never raise a hand against a woman.'

'But this attempt to patch things up clearly isn't working, is it?'

Where was the crowing? The triumphant 'I told you so's'?

'No. I really thought it might.'

A pause. I pictured her scrutinising her nails, the phone jammed between shoulder and ear, one bare brown leg flung over the side of the sofa.

'I think I may have done something stupid.'

I knew immediately what she was going to say.

'You know that journalist – the one who offered me all—'

'Yes,' I interrupted. 'You spoke to him, didn't you?'

'Well, he just kept calling and calling,' she whined. 'And I was so angry with George, getting back together with that cow when he swore he wouldn't, and so worried, you know, about me and the kids, about how we were going to manage.'

I could hear limbs being rearranged, outstretched, with that preternatural lack of modesty.

'Are you angry? You are, aren't you?'

I was a little. Gina's interview would be more than a mere prick to George's dignity. It would – must – definitively spell the end of his marriage. And from there, I knew, it would be freefall.

'Do you understand, at least, why I did it?'

People always wanted to morally validate themselves.

'Money?' I rejoined levelly.

'No, it wasn't that . . .' she snapped back. 'I didn't take the money. I wanted him back – I still do.'

'Well, there will be no chance of George and Alex getting back together after your piece comes out, that's for sure, so if that's the plan, it'll work. Just how much did you say?'

'I didn't mean to say as much as I did,' she moaned, 'but that journalist kept pushing and pushing . . .' Her anguish bounced off me. 'Have you spoken to him? I've been calling his mobile but he won't answer.'

'No, but I'm off to Forest Mere now so I'd better warn him about the piece – tell him what to expect.'

It wasn't until I put the phone down that I thought

about what the ramifications of her article would be for me.

As it happened, George and Gina's stories both appeared on the same day: two laughably jarring accounts adding yet more colour to the lurid patchwork of his public life. In titillation value Gina's far surpassed George's. She spoke of the 'rough, raw sex' she and George had enjoyed in the same Forest Mere hotel room in which he had tried to woo back his wife, during a clandestine visit that I knew nothing about.

Gina had ratcheted up the sex scenes into sumptuous sado-masochistic feasts – and I could picture the journalist, pushing, as we all do, for that killer detail. 'How did it feel when he was on top of you, holding you down? Did he pull your hair? How much noise did you both make and what did he cry out?'

George's piece didn't mention Gina until the end, temporarily reducing her to a technicality in the majestic breakdown of his marriage.

When I went back to Forest Mere that day, aware from George's kiss hello that he was drunk, there was only one aim in his mind: stripping Alex of her saintly status.

'Why am I always the villain, eh?'

'George …' We sat beside one another on the bed, gazing, not at each other but out of the French windows at a late September sky that seemed to predict the end of something. He was unshaven, in tracksuit bottoms and a T-shirt frayed around the neck, and his cheeks were crosshatched with tiny scratches. He looked like little more than a vagrant and I felt a pinch, inside, in the way that you do when hope softly implodes.

'Alex has started to drink as much as I do – she's practically rivalling me in the pisshead stakes,' he was saying, base in the narrowness of his determination to turn all his misfortune on to her. 'I'm not joking. And I always used to fight her corner, before, when people had a go at her for drinking in front of me, but now I think that, yeah,' he nodded, his posture righted by the strength of his own moral indignation, 'it does make it harder for me – of course it does. She gets almost as bad as I do when she's had a drink. Take a look at this.' Pulling up the sleeve of his T-shirt, he pointed to two bite marks, still raw, the skin ruckled away from the flesh in savage semicircles.

I had learned to tell the difference between old alcohol and the freshly ingested stuff. The strains on his breath now had the sharpness of fermented fruit, mixed in with something more gamey.

'And this.' His back was scored with scratch marks, some so deep that they had drawn blood, others bringing up the flesh in coral furrows. 'I'm going to tell people what she does to me. Show people that she's not always the victim in all this.'

'Yes, but George ...' We had been through this before. Having spent time with him, seen his behaviour good and bad, and understood that all of that was just the tiniest fraction of what Alex had witnessed, I couldn't blame her for anything. 'People will just say that you've driven her to this – that any woman would have done the same.'

But he was adamant. 'Never mind all that – this is about putting forward my side, right? And she pushes me, she really does – do you know that she's fucking Mick Hucknall? Do you?'

'I honestly don't think she is.'

'Oh, she's done worse . . .'

Saliva, had gathered, like sea foam, at the corners of his mouth; he looked rabid.

'Much worse. She thinks I don't see her flirting with men right under my nose. I'm a lot of things, but I'm no fool.'

'George, you're talking complete rubbish. You do realise that somewhere, deep down, don't you?'

But I wasn't sure he could even hear me.

'And the worst thing is I probably can't blame her for looking elsewhere . . .'

I shook my head, drained by his wild accusations.

'. . . because I haven't been able to sleep with a woman since the transplant.'

He started to giggle, a high-pitched giggle swelling up into great serrated shrieks.

'I'm impotent. Me. Isn't that just the funniest thing? Isn't that someone upstairs having a right old laugh?' His face grew serious again. 'But it can't have been much fun for Alex all this time. And now there she is thinking I've recovered, got it all back – only to get it on with some other bird. If only it were as easy as that.'

'I did wonder. I mean, all those pills. But George, you've hardly been an angel however you look at it . . .'

I thought about Gina's alleged pregnancy and the piece I needed to forewarn him about. In light of this revelation, George would probably welcome it. But it was too late to bring it up – he had moved on to other things.

'I mean do I look like someone who would hurt a woman? Do I?'

Of course he did, but I still couldn't believe it, not then.

'No.'

'Right.' He reached beneath the bed and, as though it was the most natural thing in the world, pulled out a half-empty bottle of Chardonnay. 'I swear on my life,' putting his free hand to his chest, he took a gulp, 'that I have never hit a woman; I have never hit Alex.'

His oaths, considering how little he valued his life, were meaningless and the fluency of his lies chilled me. No matter how closely I tried to seek it out, there wasn't a trace of self-doubt or bad conscience there. Over the course of the years that followed, I stopped being surprised by how many of the things he had told me weren't true and surrendered myself, not without affection, to the probability that many of his statements towards the end were a mixture of fibs and fantasy.

'I'm working really hard here, really hard. I'm still going to the gym, sometimes twice a day . . .'

I shook my head, exasperated. 'But you're drunk now, George – you're stinking drunk now.'

I couldn't even look at him. 'You tell me you love Alex, and I think you do, but why would you want to hurt her when you're the one who has done wrong? Only a week ago there you were playing happy families with Gina—'

'I've always loved women – you know that; all of them. I even had a go at you, didn't I?' he winked. 'In Malta that time . . . but you pushed me away.'

'Christ,' I smiled. George's life was collapsing around him and he was flirting.

'You're picturing it, aren't you? Being the next Mrs Best . . .'

'Oh I am.'

'So, you see: I can't help myself. I will always want to be friends with women, study them, you know? That's what I like to do. And Alex will have to accept that – and know that even if I do stop drinking for a while, there'll always be the possibility that I'll start again.'

'And what about Gina?' I still hadn't warned him about the piece due to appear that Sunday.

'Nothing ever happened with Gina. Although the other stuff,' he said, and it was the closest I ever saw him come to embarrassment, 'the other stuff is between us. I only told you because . . . well, because.'

'Right.'

'But that Gina's as good as gold,' he went on. 'She would—'

I took a deep breath. 'She's given an interview to the *News of the World*, George – told them all sorts, so you might want to rethink the whole platonic line.'

I scrutinised his face carefully as he took this in, trying and failing, as I often did, to detect genuine emotion there. There was, perhaps, only a mild self-interest in the flicker of his eyelids.

'Is it all good?'

'I expect so – she said she was pushed into saying more than she wanted, so odds are it'll be your usual eight times a night thing. She still wants to be with you so I doubt there'll be anything too damning there . . .'

He shrugged, pleased. 'Naughty girl, Gina – I always knew that.'

★   ★   ★

When the piece appeared he laughed, vanity winning out over the desire to save his marriage. He read the salacious bits aloud to me, pleased that the testosterone-fuelled maniac Gina had described to the world was him. If anything, seeing himself reflected in such a flattering sexual light reignited a desire for his former lover. He called her immediately, agreeing to go back down to Ewell where she would look after him.

Alex, by the look of the pictures in the papers, wasn't amused, telling reporters that she didn't know where her husband was and didn't care whether he came back or not. During the drive to Gina's, we both listened with interest (and, in his case, raucous amusement) to a radio phone-in questioning whether or not Alex should ever take the 'love rat' back (88 per cent said no). George heckled and applauded his supporters and dissenters from the passenger seat. 'Good girl, Debbie from Essex – good girl!'

The press followed the car in a cortège down the motorway, through Reigate and as close as they could get to Gina's house, her narrow street already densely packed with paparazzi. As I followed George into the house, quickly pulling the front door shut behind us, Gina leapt into her lover's arms, wrapping those amber legs around him with such force that he buckled, falling backwards into me.

Those squirming girls and their victorious mother had quickly rendered George impatient. Freeing himself from their embraces, he strode through into the kitchen, without so much as a glance at the outfit – tiny scalloped terry shorts and a white vest top – Gina had choreographed for his benefit. There was only one thing he wanted, and I envied him that. His was the single-mindedness of the newly in love, when every thought and action is governed by a single desire. It was the push and pull of yearning, then satisfaction. Towards the end of that summer, everything besides that one relationship with alcohol had became peripheral. The world was reduced to hinderers and abetters, and only the latter were allowed near him.

'All these women ...' Collapsed on the sofa with a little girl nestled into each side, he took a long slug from a bottle of Chardonnay. 'It's like the good old days, eh? With my two little Miss Worlds.'

'Two?' cawed Gina, before adding herself to the pile.

'All right then, three. We don't want to make your mother jealous, do we, Katie?'

Suffocated but happy, holding that bottle protectively to his chest, George called out to me.

'Come and join us!'

George drank a bottle of wine immediately. Shortly afterwards, the pair disappeared upstairs from where the occasional stifled snicker could be heard.

'Can we go upstairs and play with Mummy and Uncle George?' asked Katie finally, depositing the crescent of half-eaten Jaffa Cake on my knee.

'Not now – they'll be down soon, I'm sure.'

An hour later the children were engrossed in a children's TV series about cheerleading and I decided to leave. There was nothing to be gleaned from staying here any longer; I would come back the following day, or the one after that, to check on George's progress. Being this third person, expected to move seamlessly with his moods from Alex to Gina and her perfect family unit, was beyond what I was willing to do personally or professionally or for George.

'I'm off now, you guys, OK?' I shouted up. 'Give me a call later, George.'

Gina, dishevelled and jubilant, appeared at the top of the stairs. 'All right, my love. Drive carefully and come back soon.'

Over the next few days, the girls safely back at school, Gina gave George a taste of the life he claimed to want. In the place of the nagging and the recriminations, there was scrambled eggs on toast followed by a day-long orgy of sodden petting on the sofa, Sky Sports blazing on placidly through it all. Gina's behaviour had become more hedonistic too – a natural evolution, it seemed, for any woman caught up with George. With every visit I made, her outfits grew more brazen.

'She's the love of my life,' George slurred one night, setting his wine glass down clumsily beside a tower of Chinese take-away boxes. 'George,' I was tired of humouring him. 'Next week you'll be saying the same thing about Alex.'

'You're boring when you're like this,' he growled. 'Why don't you just piss off?'

'Can I ask you something?'

'Shoot.'

'Is all this just to get back at Alex?'

I didn't care if I annoyed him. On a binge, George was either flirty and facetious or cruel and perverse – both states conveniently masking his true feelings, so that talking to him often felt like talking to an actor in character.

'Not at all.' He sucked up some saliva, or a drop of wine he might have missed, from the sag of his bottom lip. 'I mean it. Gina never has a go at me, does she? You ever heard her say, "Oh, George, you're killing yourself." You ever heard her say that?'

'No …'

'And if you say "It's only because they care about you" …' He donned an effeminate whine and for a second I hated him.

'Don't worry, I know you're set on killing yourself.' It was hard, but I held his gaze.

'Goddamn right.' He inclined his glass in my direction in a jarring gesture of levity, but the skin around his jowls quivered.

'Where the hell's my girl, eh? Where's Gina?'

'Asleep upstairs, I think. Want me to have a look?'

He was keeping up the act well, but I knew that he wanted me out of that room.

'Sure.'

The grin was still there as I walked out, but the eyes were murderous. I didn't need to look back to know how his face would crumple as soon as I turned my back – and I got a little kick from his loathing. He was right; Gina, in all her gilded inability to see beyond the dream she was living, was the ideal – albeit unwitting – companion for this slow suicide. She could never allow herself to reproach him, not because she didn't care, but because she had to rise above George's wife in that respect in order to stay desirable. I couldn't blame her for that. Something about Gina remains touching to me to this day.

She was barefoot when I stopped by the flat later that night, dancing along to the high-pitched strains of a girl band on the radio in a fuchsia dress of some indefinable synthetic fabric, short enough to show that beneath it she was knicker-less. Through the sheer, lightly iridescent material the sharp points of her nipples were clearly visible, but the overall effect was casually exhibitionist rather than vampy. Slumped on the sofa, features plumped with hazy sensuality, George resembled a drugged chipmunk.

'Ah, the sitter's here.' He stared beyond me, beyond everything in that room. 'How do you fancy joining in, eh? We could have some fun . . .'

'Can we tell her the news, Georgie?'

Gina dropped down on to her knees at his feet, making no attempt to hide everything the action would reveal, and I averted my eyes.

'Once his divorce comes through, me and the girls are going to move in with him in Putney – start a new life together. Aren't we, Georgie?'

But I had already spotted the signs. After the declarations and grandiose promises he probably half-believed at the time, came the twitching feet and trembling fingers raked in impatient stripes through that unwashed hair. I had seen the symptoms before at Forest Mere: George was getting bored.

'I'm going to kill George when I find him,' Gina glowered, snatching the tea I hadn't quite finished and chucking it down the sink. 'He said he was going to get some things from the house late last night – it's getting cold and he doesn't have any jumpers – and that he'd be straight back. That was eight and half hours ago.'

He'd been living with her for a matter of weeks and already it was all going horribly wrong.

'If he's gone back to her,' she fixed dilated pupils on mine,

'I swear I'll ...And there'll be no taking him back when it all blows up again – I'll tell you that for nothing.'

'Calm down, Gina. He's probably on a bender in a pub somewhere making a load of new friends. You know what he's like.'

Had that been the case, I would have been there, by his side, trying to fathom which one of those 'new friends' was a journalist. As it was, Gina was right: a phone call from the desk that morning had informed me that George was at the barn with Alex, trying to woo back his beleaguered wife.

The attempt failed, Alex formally declaring the marriage over a few days later. And Gina, needless to say, did take him back. What hadn't been so easy to predict was that the groundswell of public opinion would choose that moment to turn not so much against George, as away from him. Having slowed down, then stopped and lingered for the past year and a half to observe George Best's death throes, people had suddenly, casually, tired of the carnage. Easily palatable messes are great fun, but the newspaper-reading public aren't so keen on gory close-ups. I understood this rejection of George – bored of the soap opera myself - but I was saddened by his descent into farce. Ridiculed in front rooms and pubs around Britain, his downfall had been robbed of its poignancy – and I hoped that he wasn't lucid enough to notice this shift.

With typical Irish romanticism, George I believe had always enjoyed the image of himself as a tragic genius – in his mind, it redeemed him, negating the real squalor of it all. Now, faced with the reflection of himself as a washed-up old fool, he would have nothing left. But celebrities, for us, exist solely to entertain and be judged. By the end of that summer, the entertainment had stopped and the judgements had been made. And after the expectation of his death came its anticipation.

In tune with its readers' sentiments, the paper had started to distance itself from what was now dismissed as the 'Best car crash', and I'd been assigned other, flimsier, projects to work on. By early October, only the occasional flare-up from Planet George took me back to Surrey. The last time I had been sent to find him, earlier that month, I had tracked him down to a bleak motorway pub by a service station off the M25.

There he was, a fully bearded figure standing with his back to me at the fruit machine in filthy tracksuit bottoms. He seemed smaller, somehow, and slighter, his clothing falling in folds around his shrunken frame. I experienced, for the last time, a stab of the same pathetic hope that I remembered from our first days together. I would talk to him, persuade him to go back to hospital and try again. It's to women's credit, and perhaps our detriment, that we can never quite allow ourselves to stop wanting to effect positive change. I understood then that it was the renunciation of that hope that was responsible for the deadened look in Alex's eyes.

George didn't look up when I made my approach, taking a small, theatrical sip of his spritzer before murmuring in an impassive monotone, 'Why don't you just fuck off, you little bloodsucker.'

'George – it's me. I know you probably want to be left—'

'Didn't you hear me?' He raised his head then, but there wasn't a glimmer of recognition in his eyes – just blind antipathy.

I had driven back to the office that day sure that had been our goodbye, and convinced that I didn't much care, either. Once there, I had recounted our exchange to a colleague or two with a wry amusement I didn't feel.

Given his state that day, I was astonished to hear, later that month, that Alex had agreed to give him 'one final chance' and taken him to France on what was referred to in the press as a 'make or break holiday'. A few days after their much-photographed return, Gina had announced that she was pregnant.

' "Ah well," that's all he said when I told him.' She was crying, and I heard the receiver being laid down as she blew her nose. 'Can you believe that?' she asked when she came back on.

'I can, I'm afraid.' Why couldn't she? 'But Gina, when did you find this out? You and I ... we took those tests ...'

'It *was* too early to tell.' All traces of previous emotion were gone; her voice unbreakable now. 'The doctor has confirmed that I am.'

'Gina ...'

'What?'

'I've said this before, but you do know that this won't make him come back, don't you?'

'I don't want him back,' she insisted.

I knew that I should be offering words of comfort, but on this occasion George's celebrity outweighed and corrupted everything, even the charm of the man himself.

'So?'

'So what?'

'So what am I going to do about the baby? George says he wants me to have a paternity test – can you believe that?'

'That's because he . . .' I couldn't have this conversation. 'I've got to go, Gina. Look after yourself, OK?'

A few weeks later a small piece appeared in one of the tabloids: Gina had miscarried.

There was a Sunday, not long afterwards, when George was on the front page of every single newspaper. I waded through the deluge of offensive acts he had committed – throwing a brick through one of the back windows of the barn, strewing a "symbolic circle" of fish around Gina's house, and in one rare case where he was the victim, being fleeced of £2,000 by two prostitutes – feeling something akin to admiration: how could one old drunk wreak this much havoc? Recent shots of him, bloody-knuckled and hurling abuse at some unseen demon, accompanied some of the pieces. Asked for a comment, George had replied, 'You can stick your comment up your arse.'

CHAPTER NINE

'NOTHING.'

'What do you mean, nothing?'

'Just that.'

My boss looked up from his screen, surprised to see me still standing there in his office. 'That you're to do nothing. You've been working on this story for far too long.'

'And now we're dropping it?'

'We most certainly are.' He scrabbled around for a cup on his desk which was filled with biros. 'Where are all the pencils in the world – does nobody use pencils any more?'

I cleared my throat. 'So . . .'

'Hmm? Yes. Which part of "we're dropping him" don't you get? Take some well-earned time off. Say, a week? How does that sound?'

I stared at him.

'OK, two weeks.'

'Since when have we dropped George?'

'Since early this morning, when he was caught loitering outside a primary school threatening to kill one of the mothers.'

'What?' I injected a laugh into the question, but my knees were trembling, and I looked around vainly for somewhere to sit down.

'Oh yes.' He nodded slowly to himself. 'I think that pretty much spelt the end of our special relationship. So listen: as a paper we are distancing ourselves from this mess, got it? We can report his movements – fine – but we will no longer be putting forward his point of view. He's become someone we do not wish to be associated with. How much contact do you still have with him?'

I thought about the phone calls, sometimes in the middle of the night and occasionally abusive but often no more than a slurred crossword clue or a sexually explicit joke before the line went dead. The longest conversation had been when I was getting ready for work one morning, having sent George a text message to tell him that I had finally got around to reading *The Dice Man* and could understand his fixation with it. Dark and self-destructive, the hero was a respectable man who couldn't help but take life to extremes. From George's slurred speech on the phone, I guessed that he hadn't slept. I thought about asking where he was, but once I'd heard a woman's voice begging him kittenishly to ring off, it didn't seem worth asking. Then there had been the night he had told me how much he still loved Alex, and that he wanted her back.

'He calls me, every now and again,' I said.

'Then I want you to have your phone number changed.'

'What?'

He called up his e-mails, signalling the end of the conversation.

'Don't worry about it. We'll get you another number. Does he know where you live?'

'Hang on a second: I've had that phone number for years. I can't just ... And yes, I think he does know where I live. Roughly, anyway. What is this all about?'

'Just have the number changed and talk to the travel editor about finding some nice freebie for you to go on for a couple of weeks, all right? That so hard?'

There was something else; something he wasn't telling me.

'What's he done?'

'Done?' He looked up warily. 'I've told you. Not much he hasn't done over the past few months, is there?'

He shook his head, as through trying to rid himself of an image and I realised I'd never seen him look so uncomfortable before.

'Plus, he shouldn't be calling you. And you definitely shouldn't be picking up.'

'Whatever it is he's done, I will find out, you know. So why don't you just tell me?'

He wrestled, for a moment, with something before coming out with it, eyes not moving from his screen.

'Back when you were at the barn, we'd heard that a woman was considering going to the police with an assault claim.'

I felt the air tighten around me. So that explained the appearance of the young journalist outside.

'Who is this woman?'

'No one you know. She's now gone to a paper with the story, but no one can print a word until the police have done their stuff, of course, and we're not convinced that—'

'But it's rubbish, isn't it?' I blurted out. 'Yet another woman trying to make a quick few grand out of him.'

'Quite probably.' He was looking at me curiously. 'But why are you defending him, out of interest?'

Thankfully, I wasn't given time to answer.

'George Best is a dangerous old drunk. Oh, a very charming one, I have no doubt, but none of us know what he's capable of. Having spent a month or two with the guy, on and off, at this stage in his life, doesn't give you enough of an insight into his character to be able to say what's true or not.'

He was right. Of course he was.

'Now, do as I say; take your phone down to technical, pack your bags and get out of this country for a while.'

I turned, dazed, to leave.

'Oh, and you really do look like shit. Make it somewhere sunny – it'll do you good.'

Even now, I can only remember that week alone in Spain through the filter of George. Occasionally you meet those people in life: personalities so potent that they affect the very structure of time, infecting everything on either side of your encounter. For as much as a year later, events were still being categorised as before or after George. The trip, however, did what it was supposed to: halfway through, as I lay in the winter sunshine reading a book, I realised that I hadn't thought about him once that day – until that moment.

I hadn't changed my number; there would have been no need, in any case. George hadn't called, and it wasn't until after Christmas that he made the headlines again: 'Best Arrest After Battering Wife.'

Although he was released soon after, and the charges dropped, I now accepted that there was much I had been wrong about. George was probably a wife-beater. Certainly he could be dangerous and duplicitous, a man who returned very few of the feelings of friendship he had inspired in me. Yet when I skipped straight to an article about him or turned the radio up at the mention of his name, it was with a detached affection that was there to stay. This was exaggerated in dinner party conversation, when the same question was asked again and again ('What was he really like?') and my natural instinct, out of some sense of solidarity to him, perhaps, was not to say, 'He was a violent old drunk' but to play to the gallery, keep the myth alive. And it hadn't all been a myth: George had been glorious, sharp-witted, charming – only eaten up, by the time I got to him, by his own celebrity.

It was hard to tell, from the fragments that appeared in print over the next year, how bad a state he was in. He had found a new girlfriend – more of a companion, I assumed – and although I had hoped that she might succeed in averting his death wish where the others had failed, I secretly knew that if the 'womanising' (nominal though it had become) had stopped, he was nearing the end. Girls, although secondary in his later years, something to complement the booze, had been such a strong part of his character that I registered the significance of them falling away. Everything to him now, except alcohol, was clutter. It occurred to me too that this methodical alienation of the people close to him might be a strategy: part of the concerted steps he was taking towards dying. Not out of any selfless desire to spare his nearest any pain – like all addicts George was a deeply selfish man by the end – but to enable him to concentrate on what was really important, the drinking, before slinking off quietly, like a mortally wounded animal, to die.

Even he must have known that he would never have been allowed to do that. As his inevitable deterioration became public knowledge, and he took the first steps towards disappearing for good – going missing for days, sometimes weeks at a time, always resurfacing in a seedy West London hotel or asleep in the road outside the Cheyne Walk flat he once owned – when and how he would die monopolised conversation on the radio, television and in pubs across the country.

The papers, rediscovering their interest in George now that the grand finale was drawing near, began documenting every gruesome detail. The obituaries were written – had been years ago – and the sports section was busy putting together a special colour supplement to release on the day of his funeral. As a success, he had belonged to the public; in failure he was a disaster to be relished. People looked forward to his death: only then would they be allowed to worship him again. And the fatuities came in their hundreds: 'You can't have the kind of life he had,' a BBC sports pundit told us one Saturday, 'and not lose it at the end.'

'I drove him once,' one taxi driver – a bullish set of eyes in the rear-view mirror – announced as he took me home one night, waving the front page of the *Evening Standard* ('Best: Friends Fear the End is Near') in front of the glass. 'Lovely chap: polite, funny, smart as you like.' He shook his head. 'Now, I reckon they should just put him down, like a dog with rabies, you know? Be kinder.'

I was sure I would never hear from him again, so when he rang early one Sunday morning, I thought for a moment that it was a friend playing a prank.

The Athene Hotel on the Cromwell Road was just as

238

George had described it, 'A little shithole where no one ever asks any questions.' He was right. It's the pretence that makes third-rate hotels worse than they have to be: the Pre-Raphaelite prints, rococo furniture and loud wallpaper. The Athene had none of these things. Bar a curling *FHM* calendar behind the desk, the walls of the reception area and the staircase were bare, the floor carpeted in an all-concealing burgundy carpet which, cut a little too narrow, left a dusty moat of underskirting visible.

Hypnotised by the game of blackjack on his computer screen, the receptionist handed me a key without looking up. 'He doesn't always answer the door so you'd better take this.'

A vaguely reassuring smell of instant soup emanated from one of the rooms on the first floor, and I climbed another flight of stairs up to Room 12.

The door was ajar, and I pushed it open to reveal an empty room, the bed apparently un-slept in. I wondered briefly whether I might have been directed to the wrong room. Then the sound of running water from behind the door to my left caught my attention.

'George?'

Singing, brutal and slurred as a footballer's chant, came from within.

'Half a mile from the county fair, and the rain keep pourin' down, me and Billy standin' there with a silver half a crown ...'

'George.'

'Oh, the water. Oh, the water ...'

I pushed the door a fraction.

'Are you decent?'

239

'Nope. Never have been. Who's asking?'

'It's me, George.'

'Me. Who's me?' he muttered, perplexed. 'Trouble? That you? It's bath time: come in.'

I had prepared myself for the physical implications, steeled myself for the degeneration I had noticed in recent photographs and that rancid, cider-like smell which I could conjure up by memory alone. I had expected maudlin attitudes and self-pitying declarations – all of this, but not jollity.

He was lying in the half-filled bath, wearing a dirty shirt and jeans, a bottle of white wine propped up by his head, beside the soap dish. Floating all around him, stuck to his clothing and the porcelain sides of the bath, were petals of newsprint, the disintegrating remnants of a tabloid. A full nest of mottled greys obscured George's face to two inches beneath the eyes, where the skin revealed itself to be distended like rotting fruit. There was a smear of what looked like newsprint across his temple, but he looked happy. A foul scent of wine, rose-scented soap and clogged plumbing rose, with the heat of the water, settling in a pungent slab at nose level. I reached over into the bath, turned the hot tap off and, pushing the seat of the toilet closed gingerly, sat down.

'Like the facial hair,' I nodded.

'Thanks.' Gripping the side of the bath, he pulled himself up towards me, bringing with him a whorl of hot, damp air, and rested his chin on his forearm. 'I think I've got quite a good look going on.'

'You have,' I smiled. 'Although of course most people take their clothes off before getting in the bath.'

He looked down at himself, as though realising for the first time that he was fully dressed.

'What a fucking 'eejit – would you look at that.'

He began to laugh, each rumble tumbling into the next until I had to join in. Then, amidst the dying fragments of that laughter, he began to choke.

'I'm all right, I'm all right.'

'Yeah, you look grand,' I said, in a poor imitation of his accent that drew whoops of delight.

'Do it again,' he ordered. 'Again!' Smashing his hand back down in the bath he sent water flying up into both our faces.

'George.'

'Do you wanna know something?' Folding his arms up behind his head, he leaned back into them, throwing me a patriarchal look. 'I'm pleased you and I never got involved. I am. I think it was much better this way.'

'I quite agree.'

'No.' He drew an invisible 'I won't hear of it' line through the air. 'I mean it. It would never have meant anything, anyway.'

'Thank you, George,' I flung back, scouring the room for a fresh towel with which to wipe my face. 'I'd forgotten all about that famous charm. What's amazing to me is how anyone was able to resist it.'

Astonished by such acumen, he focussed a cross-eyed stare on my mouth.

'Me too! Then again, few did and I've got myself a nice little lady now.'

A flicker of something too lucid and painful to bear passed across his features.

'You been sent to babysit?'

'No, George – you got sacked. Remember?'

'Those little bastards . . .'

The wet cotton of his shirt, stuck heavily to his shoulders and chest, had begun to constrict him and he began, with blackened jagged nails, to try to peel it off.

'Want me to . . . ?'

'Please.'

I popped open the last three buttons easily, and it floated open around him like a life jacket, revealing a stomach swollen like a infant's, that athlete's musculature for ever lost.

'Keep your eyes to yourself,' he winked, and then suddenly added, 'Why are you here? I haven't heard from you in weeks.'

'Months, George. Last time we saw each other you weren't exactly in the mood to talk. Anyway, you called me.'

'I did?'

'Yes.'

We both fell silent.

'You know that they keep expecting me to,' he donned pompous Shakespearian tones, 'shuffle off my mortal coil, don't you?'

I kept my voice even. 'I know.' Feeling I should temper this depressing fact in some way, I lied, 'But you look better than I thought you would. Far—'

'Bollocks,' he cut in with no great enthusiasm, reaching into the water and scooping up a corner of newsprint. 'They tell me it won't be long, but you know what Oscar Wilde used to say? "We're all in the gutter, but some of us are looking at the stars".'

I shook my head, conscious from the receptionist's reaction that I wasn't likely to be his only visitor during these self-imposed periods of isolation. The traffic was still passing outside, and the macabre voyeurism that was, in part, keeping me here felt increasingly wrong.

'Why do you read all that – still? After all these years does it matter so much to you what people think?'

'I don't fucking care what they think.' His voice had lost the frenzied animal-esque tone it had once taken on during similar discussions in the past. 'It's just the bollocks,' he put shrivelled fingers up to wipe his eyes, 'the sheer bollocks – and the fact that afterwards, I'll have no say. I object to that. And I object,' every word was enunciated with enormous effort, 'to the idea people seem to have that I don't know what I'm doing.' Shivering now, he focussed on me, his pupils pinpricks. 'I know exactly what I'm doing.' He leaned forward to switch the hot tap back on, prompting a small tsunami as the bath water displaced itself. 'I drink because I want to drink. I make the decision to drink, and I know that it's killing me, so I wish people would leave me to it.'

'Right.' I felt I knew all this already, though he had never put it into words.

'Oh and now, right now? I am not about to kick the bucket, so you can tell them all to stop writing their obituaries. When I do go, nobody will know about it, because I've got that part all planned: I'm going to get on a plane, and I'm not telling anyone where to. Maybe I'll go to France or Spain, to some pretty seaside town, but when I get there, I'll get a table in a bar, order a bottle of Louis XIII brandy - making sure they have enough of it in their cellar - and keep drinking until I die.'

'And the people who love you?'

'Honestly? This has got nothing to do with them. Want to know a secret?' His dimples were demonic. 'I never loved anyone as much as I love a drink. Never even came close.' He sunk down low, immersing his shoulders in the warm water. 'Fancy a spot of lunch at the Phene Arms?'

He nearly slipped twice as he climbed out of the bath, entangled in his own clothes, but half an hour later, he was lying comfortably on the hotel room's mustard bed cover with a copy of *The Dice Man* on his chest.

'Know how many times I've read this?'

'Ten, you told me. And you were right, it's good. George?'

'Hmm?'

'You going to stay here a while?'

'No,' he murmured, his eyes closing. 'I need to go and find Alex tomorrow. Need to sort things out with her – I really do. But I like it here. The curtains are ...' There was a pause and, thinking he had fallen asleep, I picked up my handbag and tiptoed to the door. As I shut it, I heard him finish the sentence, '...something special.'

Eight months later, three of which were spent on a drip in the Cromwell Hospital, the family released a picture of him to the press in a papery blue robe with tubes sticking out of his nose.

For weeks 'the greatest football legend that ever lived' was hours away from death.

'Has he kicked it yet?'

I didn't find the daily refrain at the office or the wagers taken on the precise day George was most likely to 'pop his clogs' offensive, suspecting he would be the first to laugh along with his callous fans. He'd probably place a bet of his own.

When he survived into his fourth week, I went to the Cromwell with a box of the Calippo lollies Phil had said he'd been craving and a family-sized pack of wine gums. But hospital staff, fighting every morning to get to work through the journalists and cameramen positioned outside the main entrance, had become increasingly brittle.

'You friend or family?' asked the nurse at reception.

'I'm a journalist,' I started clumsily, 'but I . . .'

'Then I'll tell you what I tell that lot every day: no journalists allowed in.'

He died at 12.55 p.m. on 25 November 2005, four weeks later, with Calum and his eighty-seven-year-old father, Dickie, at his bedside. Having guessed the date rightly, Andy, one of the subs at work, made £122 from the office sweepstake.

CHAPTER TEN

'SO GEORGE'S SISTER IS halfway through her eulogy and there we are, me and this man beside me, some old friend of George's, trying to work out roughly how many female members of the congregation he'd slept with.'

I laughed. 'And?'

'I think we decided on a conservative 60 per cent of it.'

In the three years since he died, I'd never met anyone who had attended George's funeral, never met his family, never seen Phil, Alex or Gina again. Now, I found myself at a friend's dining room table in Marylebone, beside this woman whose name I had already forgotten; this woman who had known George.

How we came on to the subject of him, I can't remember, though it never ceased to astonish me – rile me, even – how much space he still took up in every circle I chanced to move in. Almost everyone in the media world seemed to have a George Best anecdote, everyone had crossed paths with him at some point, and with every tale a more complete picture of him grew. My resentment that I had never had a chance to know that George increased accordingly.

'He would have loved knowing there were all those women, still competing over him, even at his funeral,' the woman mused, her face full of tender humour. 'Dozens of them turned up to pay their respects, some in fantastic get-ups, all of them stunning.'

Tiny fans appeared at the corners of her grey eyes with the fervour of this last sentiment, and it struck me that twenty years ago she would have been just George's type.

'I shouldn't laugh. Bits of it were terribly sad. Watching those men – George's brother and that loyal chap, his manager . . .'

'Phil.'

'That's right, Phil. Watching him carry George's coffin into the church with four of his old Man U colleagues,' she exhaled slowly, 'that got a few people going. But I liked the feeling that all of us, even as we were belting out *The Lord's My Shepherd,* were secretly thinking irreverent thoughts about him. I think what he would have really hated was to become respectable before he died. Mellowed into one of those benign old pissheads – not that there was much chance of that.'

'How did you two know each other?'

'Me?' Her voice had an ironic, macho lilt to it. 'He used to work with my ex-husband . . .'

I waited.

'And I spent one night with him twenty years ago.'

'Did you?'

She nodded, unable to repress a low giggle at her own candour.

'One of the best nights of my life, in fact.'

'Was it really?' I was fascinated. 'Go on.'

'I'd adored him for ever and ever,' she smiled, lowering her voice. 'And we knew each other a little, like I said. So then one day, on a business trip to Birmingham, I walk into a hotel bar and there he is. I was drunk after a dinner,' she added, 'very drunk. So I went up to him and said, "It's been my life's ambition to sleep with George Best." '

I pictured George twenty years ago, and the casual complacency with which he would have accepted this statement.

'So we had a drink, he took me upstairs and we made love.'

I set my wine glass down distractedly, knocking it against the side of my plate and nearly shattering the stem.

'And?'

'And it was the single most perfect experience of my life. The following morning, we had breakfast in bed and,' she shot a cautious glance at the other people around that table, 'no word of a lie, he gave me a nice little goodbye after that too. I figured things wouldn't get much better, so rather than outstay my welcome, I got dressed and was about to let myself out of the hotel room when I turned around to have one last look – you know? Check the whole thing really had happened – commit it to memory.'

I nodded, liking this woman, whoever she was.

'And this I will never forget: he was lying on his side with one leg bent, stark naked, looking straight at me, and do you know what he said?'

I shook my head.

' "Just imagine what I was like at my peak." '

ACKNOWLEDGEMENTS

I F IT WEREN'T FOR my agent, Ed Victor, who believed in *Babysitting George* before it existed, this book would never have been written. It would never have reached its current state without the vision and encouragement of Alexandra Pringle at Bloomsbury, who was able to guide me when I needed it most. Gillian Stern has known, at every stage, what was in the book's best interest; I can't thank her enough for her enthusiasm and dedication. I am similarly indebted to Anna Simpson who has patiently worked with me and always offered the best advice. Thanks too to Rob McGibbon, for the frankness of his criticism, and to Jude Drake for all her help and hard work.

When I first met Phil Hughes, all those years ago, he struck me as a novelistic hero – a loyal, kind and funny man who looked out for me over the course of that turbulent time and stayed devoted to George until his death and beyond. I would like to thank him, as well as Sharon van Geuns, Bernard Ginns and David Vincent – all of whom managed to retain their senses of humour despite everything George put us through. I am also grateful to all my colleagues at the time for their professionalism and level-headedness.

Many thanks to Stephen Purdew and Mavis Baird for sharing their many memories of George with me, and to Gina Devivo for her kindness over the course of that summer and her friendship since. I would also like to thank Alex Best and her mother Cheryl Pursey for their understanding during such a difficult time in their lives. George's sister and brother-in-law, Barbara and Norman McNarry – who decided that George's death would not be in vain and set up the George Best Foundation in 2006 – and his son, Calum, deserve a special mention.

Lastly, I would like to thank my husband for his forbearance, energy and enthusiasm, and my parents for their support and tolerance.

A NOTE ON THE AUTHOR

Celia Walden was born in Paris in 1975 and now lives in London. She is the Senior Feature Writer for the *Daily Telegraph*, *GQ Magazine*'s motoring correspondent and an interviewer for *Glamour* magazine. She is also a regular on a number of television programmes, from the *Lorraine Kelly Show* to *Sky News*. Her first novel, *Harm's Way*, was published in 2008.

A NOTE ON THE TYPE

The text of this book is set in Bembo. This type was first used in 1495 by the Venetian printer Aldus Manutius for Cardinal Bembo's *De Aetna*, and was cut for Manutius by Francesco Griffo. It was one of the types used by Claude Garamond (1480–1561) as a model for his Romain de L'Université, and so it was the forerunner of what became standard European type for the following two centuries. Its modern form follows the original types and was designed for Monotype in 1929.